VEGETARIAN
·DELIGHTS·

JUDY RIDGWAY

PIATKUS

First published in 1992 by
Judy Piatkus (Publishers) Ltd
5 Windmill St, London W1P 1HF

First paperback edition published 1993

A catalogue record for this book is available from the British Library

ISBN 0-7499-1187-5
ISBN 0-7499-1277-4 (Pbk)

Designed by Paul Saunders
Photograph opposite page 83 by Tim Imrie

Typeset in 11/12$\frac{1}{2}$ pt Linotron Sabon by
Computerset Ltd, Harmondsworth, Middlesex
Printed and bound in Great Britain by
Butler & Tanner Ltd, Frome and London

Front cover photograph shows Pasta Ribbons with
Sautéed Spring Vegetables, Chinese Money Bags, and
Fresh Ratatouille with bulgar wheat.
Back cover photograph shows Polish Egg and Dill
Soup, and Pepper and Olive Tartlets.

CANTERBURY COLLEGE

·DELIGHTS·

About the Author

Judy Ridgway has written more than two dozen books, including the international bestseller *Vegetarian Gourmet*. She was cookery editor for *Woman's World* for six years, and a wine columnist on *Women and Home* for four years. As well as writing features on food, wine, cookery and travel for a variety of newspapers and magazines, Judy appears on television and regularly takes part in national and local radio interviews and phone-ins.

Judy's other books include *The Quick After-Work Pasta Cookbook*, *The Vegetable Year*, *Salad Days*, *Vegetarian Wok Cookery*, *The Pocket Book of Oils, Vinegars and Seasonings* and *The Vitamin and Mineral Special Diet Cookbook*.

CONTENTS

———◆———

ACKNOWLEDGEMENTS

The publishers would like to thank the following organisations for supplying photographs for use in this book:

The Olive Oil Bureau (opposite page 18)
Fresh Fruit and Vegetable Information Bureau (opposite page 19)
The Pasta Information Service (opposite page 50)
Mushroom Growers' Association (opposite page 51)
Prunes from California (opposite page 82)
The American Sunflower Seed Bureau (opposite page 114)
The British Egg Information Service (opposite page 115)

Thanks also to Nice Irma's, of London W1, for the loan of props for use in the jacket photograph.

Introduction

Vegetarian food can be as enjoyable and nutritious as any other kind of food. All that is required is an adventurous spirit, and a working knowledge of the current guidelines for healthier eating.

The inspiration for the recipes in this everyday cookbook came from all the major cuisines of the world. There are soups, casseroles and pies in the Northern European tradition; curries, dhals and stir-fries from the Far East; and specialities like couscous and falafel from North Africa and the Middle East. Even more important, perhaps, is the influence of the 'Mediterranean diet', with its reliance on olive oil, garlic, fresh vegetables, beans and pasta. This diet is now thought to be the healthiest in the world.

Cooking is an art which really needs time, but how many of us home cooks can spend more than an hour or so in the kitchen? Indeed, even that amount of time often seems too long to take from the many other demands of the day. Quick pasta or rice dishes and stir-fries are the modern answer, and I have included plenty of these.

The recipes are based on fresh produce and whole grains rather than processed foods out of cans and packets. My exceptions to the use of unprocessed foods include canned tomatoes, frozen peas – where do you buy fresh ones these days? – and frozen spinach. Fresh spinach is easier to find now than it used to be, but it can be extremely expensive. You will need at least twice as much fresh spinach as frozen, possibly even three times the amount. There are a couple of recipes that do require fresh not frozen spinach, and I have indicated when this is so.

I have also used canned beans throughout. For me the convenience value outweighs any slight loss in vitamin content. This can be made up in extra fresh fruit and vegetables. (If you want to use dried beans, see page xii.)

Whole-grain products are, I believe, the best, but sometimes a more attractive result is achieved by using more processed products – 83 per cent extraction flour for instance, or, dare I say it, white flour. I have left the choice to you, giving an indication in the introduction to the recipe if a specific type of ingredient is easier to work with.

NUTRITION

The most generally accepted guidelines for healthy eating suggest that we should:

1. Eat less fat

The latest report from COMA (Committee on Medical Aspects of Food Policy) suggests that we should confine our fat intake to 33 per cent of total calories. The World Health Organisation (WHO) recommendations go even further and set the figure at 30 per cent.

For the average sedentary adult now consuming 38 per cent of total energy as fats, this means a reduction in daily intake of about 25 g (1 oz) per day. In food terms this is about 2 tablespoons of oil or a matchbox-sized amount of solid fat.

The fat which *is* eaten should be composed mainly of polyunsaturated and monounsaturated fatty acids.

These guidelines, which are based on the growing conviction that fat and particularly saturated fat plays a major part in the incidence of coronary heart disease, are not very difficult for the vegetarian to encompass. After all, saturated fats are mainly found in animal products and mono- and polyunsaturated fats are found mainly in vegetable oil.

However, saturated fats *are* found in dairy products such as milk, butter and cheese, and lacto-vegetarians do need to watch the amount of such foods that they eat. Saturated fats are also found in chocolate and, in the form of palm and coconut oil, in some cakes and biscuits, so check the ingredients listed on the label, or make your own.

Research into the effects of different kinds of fatty acids on the incidence of coronary heart disease indicates that both polyunsaturated fats such as corn and sunflower oil, and monounsaturated fats like olive and avocado oil have a beneficial effect on the cholesterol content of the blood.

The WHO recommendations set an upper limit of 7 per cent of energy on polyunsaturated fats but no upper limit on monounsaturates. However a good deal more research is required before we can decide what proportions of each would be most beneficial. In the meantime, I personally opt for a mix of polyunsaturated margarine for spreading on bread, and monounsaturated olive oil for cooking, flavouring and dressings. Olive oil is specified in a recipe if it is important for the flavour of the finished dish. Otherwise I just say 'cooking oil' and leave the choice to you. When using olive oil, extra virgin olive oil has the most flavour.

2. Eat more cereals and starchy foods

This is necessary to make up the calorie loss from eating less fat. Most vegetarians will choose to eat whole-grain cereals and indeed these products tend to be more nutritious in that there is often a substantial loss of vitamins in refined cereals.

3. Eat more dietary fibre

Fibre also has a part to play in the prevention of heart disease, as well as in diseases of the digestive tract and varicose veins. Eating whole-grain cereals such as oats and brown rice, and wholemeal bread, helps to increase the fibre content of the diet. Pulses, or dried beans and peas, and fresh fruit and vegetables also add to the total.

COMA has renamed fibre non-starch polysaccharides (NSP) which is a more exact term, and NSP is likely to appear more and more on labelling. The current target for NSP intake is 18 g (between $1/2$ and $3/4$ oz) per day. This could be provided by four slices of wholemeal bread plus 125 g (4 oz) of baked beans and a large baked potato.

4. Eat less sugar and salt

These recommendations are rather more controversial. The former is based on the fact that sugar intake plays a part in tooth decay and possibly in over-eating. The arguments against salt are based on the suggestion that high salt intake is associated with high blood pressure. This is probably true for some sections of the population, but at present scientists are unable to predict exactly who is at risk of developing high blood pressure.

5. Think about vitamin and mineral intake

For the first time COMA has looked in some detail at the requirement for specific vitamins and minerals, and new Reference Nutrient Intake (RNI) figures have replaced the old Recommended Dietary Amounts (RDA). The new figures are still not as high as the RDAs for the US, and are based on the physiological requirements of 97 per cent rather than 100 per cent of the population.

Emphasis is placed on iron – an important consideration for the vegetarian as the richest sources are animal-based. Vegetable sources include bread and breakfast cereals, dried apricots, potatoes and leafy vegetables, especially the cabbage family and watercress. Eating a vitamin C-rich food at the same meal can double the absorption of iron from a vegetable source, so orange juice with toast or blackcurrants with muesli are good combinations.

The vitamin B group and particularly B6, folic acid and B12 are also given some prominence in the COMA report. Folic acid works with vitamin B12 in the formation of red blood cells. It is found in leafy green vegetables. However, like many other vitamins it is highly unstable and can be affected by cooking and long storage.

Indeed, to make the most of any vitamin source, the food must be eaten when it is as fresh as possible and a few nutritionists go so far as to advocate eating at least one meal of raw fresh food every day.

PROBLEM AREAS

There is no reason why there should be any major problems in moving from a general to a vegetarian diet. However, there are sometimes some transitional hiccups. For example, people often step up their reliance on dairy produce thinking that they will not get sufficient protein from vegetable sources. Others find that they cannot tolerate pulses, or they put on a lot of weight through eating too much starchy food.

There should, in practice, be little difficulty with protein. We do not need anything like the current average daily intake of protein. The WHO guidelines set the lower limits for protein consumption at 10 per cent of energy or around 200 calories, and the upper limit at 15 per cent.

Of course, eggs, cheese and milk are indeed good sources of protein but they are by no means the only ones open to the vegetarian. Nuts, bread, pulses, soy products (including *tofu*) and brown rice all contain useful amounts of protein. In addition, if two or three complementary vegetable proteins are eaten together, even more protein is available to the body. Good combinations include pulses and grains, pulses and seeds and grain products and milk. Worries over the fat content of the latter are solved by using skimmed milk.

Digestive problems with pulses, and indeed an increase in fibre-rich foods generally, are usually prevented by taking things slowly. Do not suddenly inflict large quantities of unfamiliar food on the gut all at once. Build up gradually, testing your reactions as you go.

A higher intake of complex carbohydrates, such as bread and cereals, is in line with current guidelines but some first-time vegetarians overdo it and start to put on weight. The answer here is to eat more fresh fruit and vegetables. Salads can be quite filling but they do not contain the calories of rice or pasta.

HIDDEN HAZARDS

There are a few hidden hazards for the first-time vegetarian.

Cheese, for example, is usually made with rennet which is an animal product. However, more and more cheese-makers, both large and small, are beginning to offer cheese made with vegetarian alternatives. Check the labelling or ask at the delicatessen or cheese counter in the supermarket. If you have one near to you, patronise a specialist cheesemonger and ask them to stock some cheeses specially for vegetarians. The following English cheeses are made with vegetarian rennet: Ducketts Caerphilly, Devon Garland, Teifi, Tyn-Grug, Dunsyre Blue, Wealden, Cornish Yarg, Gospell Green, Gedi, Ducketts Wedmore, Wellington Cheddar, Forrester, Lanark Blue, Spenwood, and Perroche goat's cheese.

Gelatine is, of course, animal in origin, and vegetarian setting agents can be a problem to use. Gelozone is a thickener rather than a setting agent. It also needs to be boiled for 2 minutes and so is no good for setting cream or cheese-based foods or mousses with whipped egg white. Agar-agar is another vegetarian alternative which works well in place of aspic and in jellies, but it has some of the same problems as Gelozone when it comes to mousses. It also starts to set very quickly after removing from the heat and so you need to work very quickly with it. Because of the problems with these setting agents, I have avoided them completely for the recipes in this book.

Worcestershire sauce is another product which often catches out the unwary. It contains anchovies. If you like proprietary sauces, check the labels carefully.

PRACTICALITIES

Most of the ingredients used in this book can be found in the supermarket, and this includes items such as creamed coconut, vegetable stock cubes, no-soak prunes and even lemongrass. I admit, however, that it is only the larger outlets which stock the latter.

Other ingredients may need a trip to a specialist grocers or delicatessen; vine leaves from a Greek grocery store, sun-dried tomatoes and olive paste from an Italian specialist, and tamarind paste and *garam masala* from an Indian or Middle Eastern shop. Most of these specialist items are dried or bottled in oil or brine and do not take up too much space on your shelves, so stock up with a few months' supply.

Vegetable stock

Vegetable stock cubes, mentioned above, are easy to buy from all outlets and they can be pepped up with yeast extract of various kinds. To make your own vegetable stock is just as easy. I save all my vegetable cooking water, and boil it all up with a large onion, chopped (with skin on for colour), carrots, celery, bay leaf and parsley and any other vegetables which are beginning to look a bit tired. The end result is strained and frozen in ice-cube trays for use when the recipe calls for a particularly well flavoured stock.

Dried beans

As I have already said, canned beans are used throughout the book for convenience. If you want to use the dried variety you will have to plan ahead. Most require overnight soaking in plenty of cold water to make them swell. Avoid quick soaking methods using boiling water; I find that though the beans do seem to swell, they cause much more flatulence than those soaked overnight. In the interest of keeping this problem to a minimum, I would also advise throwing away all soaking water or can water.

After overnight soaking, drain and cook in fresh water. Do not add any salt at this stage as it toughens the beans. Cook in boiling water until tender. Red kidney beans *must* be boiled hard for at least 10 minutes at the start of the cooking time to get rid of the toxin they contain.

Cooking times for different beans are given opposite, but can only be an approximation as cooking times will depend on how old a bean is, how long it has been soaked and how hard the water is.

	Soaking time	Cooking time
Red kidney beans	overnight	10 minutes hard boiling plus 1 hour
Black-eye beans	overnight	1 hour
Flageolet beans	overnight	1 hour
Chick peas	overnight	$1^{1}/_{4}$ hours
Large haricot beans	overnight	$1^{1}/_{4}$ hours
Cannellini beans	overnight	$1^{1}/_{4}$ hours
Butter beans	overnight	$1^{1}/_{2}$ hours
Soya beans	at least 15 hours	2 hours

To skin tomatoes

Plunge whole tomatoes in boiling water then remove straight away. The skins will peel off easily.

To toast nuts, pine kernels and seeds

Toasting brings out the flavour of nuts, pine kernels and seeds like sesame seeds. The best way is to dry fry in a hot frying pan until lightly browned. Keep them moving in the hot pan or they will burn.

Serving quantities

All recipes throughout the book serve four unless otherwise stated.

MENU PLANNING

The traditional pattern of breakfast, lunch and dinner probably fulfils the nutritional requirements as well as any, though there is some disagreement about the relative weight of the various meals. Some experts would have you eat like a king at breakfast, a prince at midday and a pauper in the evening. Others suggest a light breakfast and supper with the main meal at midday. However, neither of these is a very convenient pattern today and the family lifestyle is dictated as much by the kids' leisure activities as by habit.

In the past the main meal of the day consisted of three courses with a central main course, usually made up of a protein with vegetables. This pattern is changing now and there is no reason why the vegetarian should not choose two or three dishes of equal weight to serve as the main course. This might be preceded by a soup and/or simply followed with fruit.

The following are some ideas for the main meal of the day, using recipes in the book. Finish with fruit, yoghurt or cheese.

Egg and Celery Soup ★ Mushroom and Walnut Risotto with green salad	Aubergine Pizza Slices ★ Cauliflower Soufflé Celery with Provence Herbs Jacket Potatoes
Zuppa di Ceci ★ Cabbage Lorraine Leeks with Cashew Nuts Jacket Potatoes	Roquefort and Celery Soup ★ Millet and Lentil Pilau Roman-Style Spinach Beetroot with Dill
Salade Ventoux ★ Pasta Ribbons with Spring Vegetables tossed salad	Stuffed Field Mushrooms ★ Greek Cheese Squares with Olives on *ciabatta* bread
Cauliflower and Grilled Red Pepper Salad ★ Bean and Cabbage Soup with Wholemeal Rolls	Bitter Salad with Grilled Red Peppers ★ Malaysian Vegetable Fruit Curry Spiced Potatoes or Yams
Gazpacho ★ Courgettes with Pine Kernels and Orange Broad Beans in *Tahina* Sauce Fried Noodles with Watercress	Cabbage and Onion Casserole Baked Sweet Potatoes Lettuce with Spring Onions and Peas ★ Marinated Brie with Wholemeal Rolls

The First-or Only-Course

SOUPS

Home-made soups knock spots off the canned or packet variety. They taste delicious, are not very onerous to make, and will store well. There are only a few, such as Polish Egg and Dill Soup and *Miso* Soup, which need to be made at the last minute.

I try to make double quantity of any recipe, and thus usually have a choice of two or three soups in store. Freeze in single or double portions for the most flexibility. The Egg and Celery Soup should be frozen without the eggs and tomato, but the rest will freeze well.

Soups like Bean and Cabbage Soup, Polish Egg and Dill Soup, Zuppa di Ceci, Vegetable Gumbo, and Lentil and Watercress Soup make filling main-course dishes served with plenty of wholemeal bread or with a dollop of brown rice.

Curried Parsnip Soup

Almost any root vegetable except perhaps beetroot can be substituted for parsnips in this recipe. The light curry flavour adds an extra dimension.

1 large onion, peeled and sliced
1 tablespoon cooking oil
450g (1lb) parsnips, peeled and
  chopped
1 tablespoon curry powder

salt and freshly ground black
  pepper
900ml (1½ pints) vegetable stock
  (see page xii)

1. Fry the onion in the cooking oil until lightly browned. Add the parsnips and curry powder and continue frying for 2-3 minutes.

2. Add the seasoning and stock and bring to the boil. Cover and simmer for 30 minutes until the parsnips are tender.

3. Purée in a blender or food processor or rub through a sieve, and reheat before serving.

Roquefort and Celeriac Soup with Croûtons

——◆——

Celeriac gives a distinctive but delicate flavour to this soup. If you cannot find it, celery can be used instead but you will need to add a large potato to ensure a good texture.

1 tablespoon cooking oil
15g (¹/₂oz) butter
2 onions, peeled and sliced
450g (1lb) celeriac, peeled and chopped
1 carrot, peeled and chopped
750ml (1¹/₄ pints) vegetable stock (see page xii)
freshly ground black pepper

150ml (¹/₄ pint) single cream
125g (4oz) Roquefort cheese, crumbled

Croûtons
2 slices of white bread, crusts removed
25g (1oz) softened butter or vegetable oil

1. Heat the oil with the butter and gently fry the onion, celeriac and carrot for 3-4 minutes to bring out the flavours. Add the vegetable stock and pepper and bring to the boil. Cover and simmer for 30 minutes.

2. Rub through a sieve or purée in a blender or food processor.

3. Return to the saucepan and add the cream and cheese. Carefully reheat without boiling, stirring all the time, until the cheese melts.

4. **To make the croûtons,** spread the butter, if using, over each side of the slices of bread. Cut into fingers and fry on both sides until crisp. Dice and use to garnish the soup.

To make garlic croûtons, mash the butter with crushed garlic before spreading on the bread.

Egg and Celery Soup

—◆—

The flavour of this Italian soup is much stronger than you would expect given the simplicity of the ingredients. This is due to the sweetness of the vegetables and the flavour of the olive oil.

SERVES 6

2 large onions, peeled and coarsely chopped
1 head of celery, washed and sliced
2 tablespoons extra virgin olive oil
750ml (1¼ pints) strong vegetable stock (see page xii)
salt and freshly ground black pepper

3 tomatoes, skinned (see page xiii) and halved
3 hard-boiled eggs, peeled and quartered
4 tablespoons freshly chopped parsley

1. Gently fry the onions and celery in the oil for 2-3 minutes to soften slightly. Add the stock and seasoning and bring to the boil. Cover and simmer for 30 minutes.

2. Add the tomatoes and eggs and return to the boil for 2 minutes.

3. Ladle into soup bowls making sure that everyone has half a tomato and two pieces of egg. Sprinkle with the chopped parsley.

Pepper and Marrow Soup

—◆—

I am a great marrow lover. I like them stuffed with flavoured rice or cracked wheat, baked with onions and tomato, or steamed with fresh dill. In season a good marrow is often so large that it can be used for more than one dish and still have something left over. This is a good way of using up part of a large vegetable marrow.

4

600g (1¹/₄lb) piece of marrow,
    peeled and seeded
2 medium courgettes, trimmed
2 sweet peppers (preferably 1 red
    and 1 green), seeded
2 tablespoons cooking oil

1 small bunch of chives, 2-3 spring
    onions or a peeled shallot
2 sprigs of fresh basil, if available
salt and freshly ground black
    pepper
900ml (1¹/₂ pints) water

1. Chop the flesh of the marrow, courgettes and peppers.

2. Heat the oil in a pan and add the vegetables. Sweat over a gentle heat for 5 minutes or so. Add all the remaining ingredients and bring to the boil. Cover and simmer for 30 minutes.

3. Rub through a sieve or purée in a blender or food processor. Reheat and serve.

Brussels Sprout and Chestnut Soup

—◆—

This traditional combination of Brussels sprouts and chestnuts makes a subtle soup. If using canned chestnuts, check to see that they are not sweetened!

1 onion, peeled and chopped
1 tablespoon cooking oil
50ml (2 fl oz) dry sherry
450g (1lb) Brussels sprouts, sliced
125g (4oz) chestnuts, peeled and
    sliced, or 75g (3oz) whole
    canned chestnuts, drained

300ml (¹/₂ pint) milk
600ml (1 pint) vegetable stock (see
    page xii)
salt and freshly ground black
    pepper
4 tablespoons single cream

1. Fry the onion in cooking oil until it turns translucent. Add the sherry and bring to the boil.

2. Add all the remaining ingredients except the cream and return to the boil. Simmer for 20 minutes until the vegetables and chestnuts are tender.

3. Purée in a blender or food processor or rub through a sieve. Reheat and serve with a swirl of cream in each dish.

Tomato, Cauliflower and Tarragon Soup

In my opinion, the butter and sherry in this delightful soup are essential to the flavour, but olive oil and dry white wine could be used instead.

25g (1 oz) butter
1 onion, peeled and chopped
75ml (3 fl oz) dry sherry
225g (8 oz) cauliflower, chopped
225g (8 oz) tomatoes, chopped
750ml (1¼ pints) vegetable stock
(see page xii)

2-3 tablespoons freshly chopped
tarragon, or 1 teaspoon dried
tarragon
½ teaspoon sugar
salt and freshly ground black
pepper

1. Melt the butter in a pan, add the onion, and gently fry until golden in colour.

2. Add the sherry and bring to the boil. Add all the remaining ingredients and simmer for 35 minutes.

3. Rub through a sieve or process to a purée. Correct seasoning if necessary and serve sprinkled with a little more fresh tarragon.

Jerusalem Artichoke Soup

Try this interesting Dutch soup with garlic croûtons (see page 3). The recipe comes from some friends in The Hague who say that the garlic helps to bring out the flavour of the artichokes.

1 small onion, peeled and chopped
1 tablespoon cooking oil
350g (12 oz) Jerusalem artichokes,
washed
2 carrots, peeled and chopped

2 tomatoes, chopped
600ml (1 pint) vegetable stock (see
page xii)
salt and freshly ground black
pepper

1. Fry the onion gently in the oil.

2. Meanwhile peel the artichokes, wash again, chop and add to the pan. Work as quickly as possible as they turn black very quickly.

3. Add the remaining ingredients. Bring to the boil, cover and simmer for 30 minutes.

4. Rub through a sieve or purée in a blender or food processor. Reheat and serve.

Apple and Celery Soup
—◆—

This fruit-based soup actually comes from Germany, but it is typical of many parts of eastern Europe. In Germany it is served hot with a garnish of small ratafia biscuits.

SERVES 12

25g (1 oz) butter
3 onions, peeled and chopped
150ml (¼ pint) dry sherry or white vermouth
700g (1½lb) cooking apples, cored and chopped
700g (1½lb) celery, trimmed and chopped

2.5 litres (4 pints) water
2 teaspoons ground cumin
salt and freshly ground black pepper
150ml (¼ pint) soured cream

1. Melt the butter in a pan and fry the chopped onion until softened. Add the sherry or vermouth and bring to the boil.

2. Add the chopped apple and celery, and the water. Sprinkle with cumin and seasoning and bring to the boil. Simmer for 45 minutes.

3. Purée in a blender or food processor. Add soured cream and reheat before serving.

Lentil and Watercress Soup

——◆——

This is a lovely warming soup, ideal for winter weather. If you are in a hurry omit the whole green lentils – the flavour will be just as good but the texture will not be as interesting.

SERVES 6-8

1 tablespoon olive oil
1 medium onion, peeled and sliced
450g (1lb) carrots, peeled and
   chopped
75g (3 oz) red split lentils, picked
   over
3 large vegetable stock cubes
1.2 litres (2 pints) boiling water
2 sprigs of fresh parsley

1 sprig of fresh thyme, or $\frac{1}{4}$
   teaspoon dried thyme
1 bay leaf
salt and freshly ground black
   pepper
75g (3 oz) watercress, stalks and all
25g (1 oz) whole green lentils

1. Heat the oil in a pan and fry the onion until it begins to turn brown. Add the carrot and cook over a very low heat for 3-4 minutes, stirring all the time. Add the split lentils, stock cubes, boiling water, herbs and seasoning, and bring to the boil. Reduce the heat and simmer for 30 minutes.

2. Remove the sprig of thyme and the bay leaf. Add the watercress and cook a further 5 minutes. Process in a blender or food processor or rub through a sieve.

3. Return to the heat and add the whole lentils. Simmer for a further 30 minutes until the whole lentils are just cooked.

Vegetable Gumbo
—◆—

Louisiana is the traditional home of this filling soup. It can be made with a variety of ingredients but traditionally it should always contain okra and Tabasco sauce. Go easy on the latter or the soup will be very hot indeed!

1 large onion, peeled and chopped
1 garlic clove, peeled and crushed
  (optional)
2 sweet peppers (1 red and 1
  green), seeded and chopped
2 tablespoons corn oil
1 × 225g (8 oz) can of tomatoes
175g (6 oz) baby corn
4-5 celery sticks, trimmed and
  sliced

600ml (1 pint) strong vegetable
  stock (see page xii)
salt and freshly ground black
  pepper
a few drops of Tabasco sauce (to
  taste)
75g (3 oz) long-grain American rice
225g (8 oz) okra, washed and
  trimmed

1. Fry the onion, garlic (if using), and pepper in the oil for 3-4 minutes. Add the contents of the can of tomatoes and all the remaining ingredients except the rice and okra. Bring to the boil and simmer for 20 minutes.

2. Meanwhile put the rice in a saucepan with double its volume of salted boiling water. Cover and simmer for 13-14 minutes until all the liquid has been absorbed and the rice is tender.

3. Add the okra to the simmered vegetables and cook gently for a further 10 minutes. Gentle simmering is required to stop the okra from splitting.

4. To serve, place small mounds of rice in each soup bowl and carefully spoon the soup around the rice.

Zuppa di Ceci

—◆—

This version of Italian chickpea soup is typical of Lombardy. In other areas carrots and celery are also included, but I feel they are unnecessary because of the wonderful flavour of the mushrooms. If fresh sage is not available, use ¼ teaspoon dried sage instead, and add with the salt and pepper.

15g (¹/₂ oz) dried Italian mushrooms or ceps
1 large onion, peeled and coarsely chopped
2 garlic cloves, peeled and crushed
2 tablespoons olive oil
1 × 400g (14 oz) can of chickpeas, drained

1 tablespoon flour
750ml (1¹/₄ pints) vegetable stock (see page xii)
1 teaspoon tomato purée
salt and freshly ground black pepper
6-8 Cos lettuce leaves, shredded
1 sprig of fresh sage

1. Put the mushrooms to soak in just enough boiling water to cover them.

2. Fry the onion and garlic in the oil until lightly browned.

3. Toss the drained chickpeas in flour and add to the pan with the mushrooms and their soaking water, the stock, tomato purée and seasoning. Bring to the boil and simmer for 15-20 minutes.

4. Add the lettuce and sage and simmer for 1 minute more. Serve at once with a little extra virgin olive oil poured into the soup.

Hungarian Apple Soup

—◆—

I first encountered this unusual, slightly sweet soup on a visit to Lake Balaton in Hungary. It was the speciality of one of the lakeside restaurants, and was served with large chunks of rye bread.

2 onions, peeled and chopped
1 garlic clove, peeled and chopped
4 eating apples, cored and diced
1 red pepper, seeded and chopped
2 large gherkins or 1 pickled
   cucumber, diced
2 tablespoons cooking oil

750ml (1¹/₄ pints) vegetable stock
   (see page xii)
¹/₂ teaspoon paprika
2 tablespoons chopped chives
125ml (4 fl oz) soured cream
50g (2 oz) fine breadcrumbs
   (optional)

1. Gently fry the onion, garlic, apple, red pepper and gherkin in the cooking oil. After 3-4 minutes add the stock and paprika. Bring to the boil and simmer for 20 minutes.

2. Remove from the heat and stir in half the chives and the soured cream. Serve sprinkled with more chives.

3. For a slightly thicker soup stir in the fresh breadcrumbs.

Miso Soup

——◆——

This traditional Japanese soup uses seaweed, *tofu* and *miso*. Dried seaweed and *Miso*, a fermented bean paste, are on sale in most health-food stores. It is important not to overcook *miso*, so do not add until just before serving and do not allow the soup to boil after you have added it.

25g (1 oz) dried Japanese seaweed
750ml (1¹/₄ pints) well flavoured
   vegetable stock (see page xii)
1 tablespoon miso

125g (4 oz) tofu or beancurd, sliced
6 spring onions, trimmed and
   sliced

1. Reconstitute the seaweed as directed on the packet.

2. Heat the stock in a saucepan and add the seaweed and its soaking water. Bring to the boil and cook the seaweed for the time directed on the packet.

3. Remove from the heat and stir in the *miso*.

4. Divide the *tofu* and spring onions between four soup bowls and pour on the soup. Serve at once.

Bean and Cabbage Soup

——◆——

This recipe is based on an Italian recipe called *Ribollita* which is made with black cabbage and rather more beans! In Italy it is cooked until it is quite thick and then ladled on to thick hunks of bread to serve.

SERVES 4-6 as a main course

1 medium onion, peeled and finely
   chopped
1 garlic clove, peeled and finely
   chopped
1 small fresh sprig of rosemary
1 fresh bay leaf
1 tablespoon olive oil
2 sticks of celery, trimmed and
   thinly sliced
1 carrot, peeled and finely diced

1 tablespoon tomato purée
1.8 litres (3 pints) well flavoured
   vegetable stock (see page xii)
400g (14 oz) can of cannellini or
   haricot beans, drained
1/2 small to medium Savoy cabbage
   (450 g/1lb when trimmed),
   shredded
salt and freshly ground black
   pepper

1. Gently fry the onion, garlic, rosemary and bay leaf in the oil for 3-4 minutes. Add the celery and carrot and continue cooking for a further 5 minutes to soften, but not to brown.

2. Remove the herbs and add the tomato purée and stock. Bring to the boil and simmer for 15 minutes.

3. Rub half of the beans through a sieve and add to the soup with the other half of the beans, whole, and the cabbage. Check seasoning and simmer for a further 10 minutes.

Iced Cucumber Soup

—◆—

The delicate flavour of this soup is best appreciated when it is chilled.

25g (1 oz) butter, or 1¹/₂
   tablespoons cooking oil
1 medium onion, peeled and sliced
150ml (¹/₄ pint) dry white wine
225g (8 oz) potatoes, peeled and
   sliced
¹/₂ large cucumber, chopped
600ml (1 pint) vegetable stock (see
   page xii)

salt and freshly ground black
   pepper

Garnish
2.5 cm (1 in) cucumber, diced
4 tablespoons plain yoghurt or
   single cream
parsley or chervil sprigs

1. Heat the butter or oil in a pan and fry the onion till golden. Add the wine and bring to the boil. Add the potatoes, cucumber, vegetable stock and seasoning. Simmer for 30 minutes, then allow to cool.

2. Liquidise and correct seasoning if necessary. Leave to cool then chill in the fridge. To serve, garnish with a swirl of yoghurt or cream, diced cucumber and sprigs of chervil or parsley.

Chilled Beetroot Soup

—◆—

The soured cream gives this soup a pretty marbled effect.

1 medium onion, finely chopped
1 garlic clove, peeled and crushed
25g (1 oz) butter or firm margarine
3 medium cooked beetroots,
   skinned and roughly chopped

600ml (1 pint) vegetable stock (see
   page xii)
salt and freshly ground black
   pepper
150ml (¹/₄ pint) soured cream

1. Fry the onion and garlic in the butter or margarine until softened but not browned. Add the beetroot, stock and seasoning and bring to the boil. Simmer for 5 minutes.

2. Liquidise until smooth and allow to cool. Chill for at least 4 hours. Before serving, stir in the soured cream to give a marbled effect.

Chilled Fennel Soup

—◆—

The use of fennel has a surprisingly lengthy history in the UK, although we associate it mainly with Italy. This unusual recipe is actually based on one which was popular as long ago as the fourteenth century. You may be surprised to discover that it is thickened with ground almonds

1 large or 2 smaller heads of Italian fennel, trimmed
450ml (³/₄ pint) water
125ml (4 fl oz) dry white wine

salt and freshly ground black pepper
25g (1 oz) ground almonds
150g (5 oz) plain yoghurt

1. Retain a little of the feathery green parts of the head of fennel and coarsely chop the rest. Place in a pan with the water, wine and seasoning. Bring to the boil, cover and simmer for 30 minutes.

2. Rub the soup through a sieve or purée in a blender or food processor. Return to the pan and stir in the ground almonds. Bring back to the boil and simmer for a further 15 minutes, stirring from time to time. Remove from the heat and leave to cool.

3. Blend in the yoghurt and chill for at least 30 minutes before serving with the finely chopped green feathery parts of the fennel sprinkled over the top.

Polish Egg and Dill Soup

—◆—

This soup has a lovely texture with the smooth yoghurt contrasting with the crunchy vegetables. It's quick to prepare, and you can add almost any flavourings. Try tomato and basil in place of the eggs and dill. Serve as a main course with crusty Wholemeal Rolls (see page 128).

10 cm (4 in) cucumber, thinly sliced
2 carrots, peeled and grated or finely shredded
4 tablespoons freshly chopped dill
600g (1¹/₄lb) low-fat plain yoghurt
4 hard-boiled eggs, roughly chopped

12-16 fresh spinach leaves, finely shredded
salt and freshly ground black pepper
sprigs of dill

1. Cut the cucumber slices in half and retain a few for garnish along with some grated or shredded carrot.

2. Place all the remaining ingredients in a large bowl and mix well together. Chill for half an hour.

3. Serve in individual bowls garnished with the retained cucumber, carrots and sprigs of dill.

Gazpacho

The riper the tomatoes the better this wonderful cold Spanish soup will taste. Plum or beef tomatoes often have the most flavour, and are increasingly available.

1 kg (2lb) very ripe tomatoes, skinned (see page xiii) seeded and chopped
1 red pepper, seeded and chopped
7.5 cm (3 in) cucumber, diced
2 tablespoons finely chopped spring onion
1 teaspoon freshly chopped garlic
5 tablespoons cider or wine vinegar

4 tablespoons extra virgin olive oil
1$\frac{1}{2}$ tablespoons tomato purée
175-250ml (6-8 fl oz) water

Garnishes
$\frac{1}{2}$ red pepper, seeded and diced
$\frac{1}{2}$ green pepper, seeded and diced
5 cm (2 in) cucumber, diced

1. Place the chopped tomato, red pepper, cucumber, spring onion and garlic in a blender or food processor with the vinegar. Blend until smooth.

2. Stir in the remaining ingredients and chill for 1 hour.

3. Prepare the garnishes just before serving and place in separate bowls, for guests to sprinkle on to their soup themselves.

STARTERS

The recipes in this section do indeed make a good start to the meal, but many of them can be adapted to serve as snacks or light main-course dishes. Try Mushroom and Fennel Salad or Shropska in pitta bread parcels, for example, or add some Mozzarrella cheese to the Grapefruit and Avocado Salad or the Three-Fruit Salad, or increase the quantities of *fromage frais* in the Avocado and Orange Platter.

Mushrooms and Chickpeas à la Grecque can be served hot with jacket potatoes, and Salade Ventoux goes well with other salads. Japanese Fried Beancurd, Aubergine Pizza slices, and Stuffed Field Mushrooms and Stuffed Mediterranean Aubergines can all be increased in quantity to make more substantial dishes.

Mushroom and Fennel Salad

The flavours of these two vegetables complement each other particularly well. Serve as a starter on a bed of lettuce or turn it into a more elaborate dish by adding melon balls.

2 small heads or 1 large head of
  Italian fennel, trimmed
salt and freshly ground black
  pepper
175g (6oz) button mushrooms,
  quartered or chopped

4 tablespoons mayonnaise
a pinch of dried thyme or mixed
  herbs
1 small Ojen melon, seeded and
  scooped into balls (optional)
salad leaves

1. Blanch the trimmed heads of fennel in a little boiling salted water for 3-4 minutes, or steam for 5-6 minutes in a steamer. Drain, cool and chop.

2. Mix with all the other ingredients. Serve on a bed of salad leaves.

Grapefruit and Avocado Salad

—◆—

Fried breadcrumbs add texture to this simple and refreshing salad. Pink grapefruit are usually sweeter than the ordinary grapefruit. Choose according to how astringent you like your first course to be.

1 slice of wholemeal bread
1 bunch of parsley
salt and freshly ground black
*   pepper*
2 tablespoons olive oil
2 grapefruit, peeled and segmented
*   (retaining the juice)*
2 avocados, halved, stoned and
*   peeled*

small sprigs of fresh oregano, basil
*   and continental parsley*

Dressing
3 tablespoons extra virgin olive oil
2 teaspoons red wine vinegar

1. Process the bread and parsley in a blender or food processor to chop finely. Mix with plenty of seasoning. Heat the oil in a frying pan and add the breadcrumb mixture. Fry slowly until well browned all over, stirring all the time to ensure even browning.

2. Arrange the grapefruit segments in the centre of four serving plates. Slice the avocado and place a slice between each grapefruit segment. Sprinkle with breadcrumb mixture. Roughly chop herbs and sprinkle on top.

3. Mix the retained grapefruit juice with the oil and vinegar and some salt and pepper, and pour over the salads. Serve at once.

Artichokes with Briarde Dressing

—◆—

This is my favourite dressing for large French globe artichokes. Its fresh and piquant flavour seems to match that of the artichoke very well.

Knock off the stems before cooking the artichokes, hitting them with a rolling pin or hammer. The stems will come off with long stringy bits attached to them, whereas if you cut them off with a knife these bits remain in the heart of the artichoke.

4 large globe artichokes, stems
  removed (see above)
1 lemon, sliced
225g (8oz) fromage frais or quark
  low-fat soft cheese
2 tablespoons milk or water
1 tablespoon red wine vinegar

4-5 radishes, trimmed and finely
  chopped
3-4 gherkins, finely chopped
1 tablespoon freshly chopped basil
salt and freshly ground black
  pepper

1. Boil the artichokes in a large pan of water with the sliced lemon. This will help the vegetables to retain their colour. Cook for about 45 minutes until very soft in the base. Drain and leave to cool, then remove and discard the centre leaves and the hairy choke.

2. Blend the *fromage frais*, milk or water and vinegar to a smooth cream. Stir in all the remaining ingredients and serve with the cold cooked globe artichokes.

opposite: Garlic Sauce with Vegetables (page 172) and Tapenade with toasted bread (page 170)

facing page 19: Vegetable Terrine (page 154)

Marinated Courgettes

—◆—

This dish from Provence can be kept in the fridge for a day or two, and it improves each day. The flavour depends very much on the use of sage although this is not typical of the region.

2 large courgettes, about 350g (12 oz) in total weight
4 tablespoons olive oil
salt and freshly ground black pepper

1 garlic clove, peeled and chopped
1 tablespoon chopped sage leaves, or 1 teaspoon dried sage
1 tablespoon red wine vinegar
150ml (1/4 pint) dry white wine

1. Top and tail the courgettes and cut into thick slanting slices. Heat 2 tablespoons olive oil in a frying pan and lightly brown the courgette slices on each side. Pack into a pâté dish, seasoning each layer.

2. Pour the remaining oil into the pan and fry the garlic and sage until the garlic is brown. Add the vinegar and wine and bring to the boil.

3. Pour the hot liquid over the courgettes so that the courgettes are fully covered. Cover with foil and place in the fridge when cold. Leave to chill for at least an hour before serving.

Avocado and Orange Platter

—◆—

Avocado mixes well with all citrus fruit, and although this recipe uses oranges, you could just as easily use grapefruit. Make just before serving or the avocados will discolour.

2 large oranges, peeled and sliced into rounds
2 large avocados, peeled, stoned and sliced into lengths

4 tablespoons quark *low-fat soft cheese*
1 tablespoon cashew nuts, chopped
1 tablespoon raisins, chopped

1. Arrange the orange rounds on four individual plates and place two or three slices of avocado between them.

2. Mix the remaining ingredients together and place a spoonful in the centre of each plate. Serve at once.

Vinaigrette Vegetables

—◆—

Wherever you go on the Mediterranean coast – in Italy, Spain and France – you will find a version of this recipe.

All kinds of vegetables can be cooked, coated with a well flavoured vinaigrette while still warm, then chilled. Here are some ideas. There is no reason why you should not mix and match the vegetables and dressings to suit your own particular tastes, though I can strongly recommend the Honey Vinaigrette on fennel, and the Walnut and Tarragon Vinaigrette on courgettes.

Vegetables from which to choose:

450g (1lb) steamed and sliced courgettes or
steamed whole baby leeks or
steamed and sliced fennel or
sliced and grilled aubergines or
seeded and grilled red peppers

Dressings:

1. French Vinaigrette
6 tablespoons olive oil
1¹/₂ tablespoons red wine vinegar
salt and freshly ground black pepper
a little mustard (optional)

2. Walnut and Tarragon Vinaigrette
6 tablespoons walnut oil
2 tablespoons tarragon vinegar
1 teaspoon freshly chopped shallots or spring onions
salt and freshly ground black pepper

3. Honey Vinaigrette
6 tablespoons olive oil
1 tablespoon cider vinegar
2 teaspoons clear honey
1 teaspoon grainy mustard
salt and freshly ground black pepper

Guacamole-Stuffed Tomatoes
——◆——

Use the recipe on page 161 to make this smooth Mexican avocado dip, and use it as the Spanish do, to stuff tomatoes. You will need about half quantity to fill four large tomatoes.

¹/₂ quantity Guacamole
  (see page 161)
4 continental tomatoes

salt and freshly ground black
  pepper
sprigs of fresh coriander

1. Make up the Guacamole and cover with clingfilm until required.

2. Slice the tops off the tomatoes and discard. Dig out the centre seeds with a teaspoon and discard.

3. Season the inside of the tomatoes and spoon in the Guacamole. Garnish with sprigs of fresh coriander.

Shropska
——◆——

The fresh, clean taste of this crunchy Bulgarian salad makes it a very good summer dish. I usually serve it as a first course, but it could also be served as a side salad.

4 large tomatoes
1 small onion, peeled
¹/₂ green pepper, seeded
10 cm (4 in) cucumber
3-4 sticks of celery

salt and freshly ground black
  pepper
125g (4oz) Cheddar cheese, grated
juice of 1 lemon

1. Coarsely chop all the vegetables and layer in individual bowls. Season and top with grated cheese and lemon juice.

2. Chill for half an hour before serving.

Three-Fruit Salad

—◆—

One tends to think of 'fruit salad' as a dessert, but this mixture makes a very good first course or lunch snack. Buy the best balsamic vinegar you can afford, as some of the cheaper ones don't have the characteristic full fruity flavour.

2 kiwi fruit, peeled and sliced
2 Sharon fruit, sliced
2 tomatoes, sliced
a few mixed salad leaves
2 tablespoons pine kernels, toasted
  (see page xiii)
1 tablespoon small black olives

sprigs of fresh parsley

Dressing
5 tablespoons extra virgin olive oil
1/2 teaspoon balsamic vinegar
salt and freshly ground black pepper

1. Arrange the three sliced fruits in an overlapping rosette on four plates. Place a few mixed leaves round the outside. Place pine kernels and black olives at intervals and dot with parsley.

2. Mix all the dressing ingredients together and sprinkle all over the salad, but particularly on the fruit.

Chickpeas à la Grecque

—◆—

I stumbled on this excellent variation of Mushrooms à la Grecque when I was thinking of ideas for using up some canned chickpeas. They give an interesting texture to this traditional dish, but you could of course revert to the original by leaving them out and adding more button mushrooms.

2 small onions, peeled and sliced
4 tablespoons olive oil
225g (8oz) button mushrooms
125g (4oz) canned chickpeas,
  drained
600ml (1 pint) dry white wine
2 teaspoons tomato purée

1/2 teaspoon dried oregano
1 bay leaf
1/4 teaspoon fennel or coriander
  seeds
salt and freshly ground black pepper

22

1. Fry the onion in 2 tablespoons of the olive oil until transparent. Add the mushrooms, halved if necessary, and chickpeas. Pour over the wine and add all the other ingredients. Bring to the boil and simmer for 30 minutes.

2. Serve chilled.

Salade Ventoux

I came across this delicious use of goat's cheese and olive oil on a visit to the Provence olive oil harvest one December. The sun was shining but it was quite cold, and this warm salad made a great lunchtime starter. It is of course just as good in the evening!

4 small green peppers, quartered and seeded
225g (8oz) soft goat's cheese, skin removed
8 tablespoons extra virgin olive oil

3 tablespoons plump raisins
2 tablespoons pine kernels, toasted (see page xiii)
1 teaspoon balsamic vinegar

1. Place the peppers, skin side up under a hot grill and cook until well charred. Transfer to a soup bowl and cover with a plate. Leave to stand for half an hour and then peel.

2. Cut the cheese into four thick slices and place in a warm, not hot, oven.

3. Heat the oil in a pan with the raisins until they just begin to sizzle. Add the pine kernels and vinegar and remove from the heat.

4. Arrange the peppers on four warm plates. Add the cheese and spoon the olive oil mixture over the top of both. Serve at once.

Fried Kale with Almonds

—◆—

Treated in this way, curly kale tastes exactly like deep-fried 'seaweed' served in Chinese restaurants – not surprising really, since it is in fact cabbage and not seaweed that they use. Serve it as a starter as part of a Chinese-style meal or an accompaniment with other vegetables.

150-175g (5-6oz) curly kale
2 tablespoons flaked almonds

cooking oil

1. Remove the stalks and shred the curly kale very finely. Mix with the flaked almonds.

2. Pour about 1 cm (½ in) of cooking oil into the bottom of a large heavy-based pan. Heat until very hot. Drop half the kale mixture into the pan and stir. Take care as the fat will splash a little.

3. When all the kale is crispy – this happens very quickly – remove with a slotted spoon and drain on kitchen paper. Repeat the process with the remaining kale mixture. Drain and serve at once.

Love Apples

—◆—

It took me three tries before I managed to reproduce this delicious special-occasion starter which I first tasted in a restaurant in the Conway valley in North Wales. The cheese and cream should not be added too soon, because you want the end result to be runny rather than set.

8 tomatoes, peeled (see page xiii) and sliced
250-300ml (8-10fl oz) dry or medium dry sherry

salt and freshly ground black pepper
25g (1oz) Cheddar cheese, grated
50ml (2fl oz) double cream

1. Preheat the oven to 180°C/350°F/Gas 4.

2. Divide the sliced tomatoes between four small ramekin dishes. Pour in enough sherry to cover, and season. Bake in the oven for 20 minutes.

3. Sprinkle each dish with grated cheese and cream, and continue cooking for a further 4-5 minutes. Serve at once.

Japanese Fried Beancurd

—◆—

This is a classic Japanese way of serving fresh beancurd or *tofu*. It is often served on its own as an additional course between the soup and the main dishes. If you cannot find the *miso*, increase the amount of light soy sauce to 75 ml (3 fl oz) and reduce the water to 25 ml (1 fl oz).

300g (10oz) tofu
1 tablespoon sunflower oil
25ml (1fl oz) light soy sauce, or 1 tablespoon ordinary soy sauce
25ml (1fl oz) rice vinegar or medium sherry

1 teaspoon grated root ginger
125ml (4fl oz) water
1 teaspoon miso
2 spring onions, finely chopped

1. Cut the *tofu* into four rectangular pieces. Heat the oil in a non-stick frying pan and fry the *tofu* on all sides to seal. Place in small individual bowls.

2. Heat the soy sauce, rice vinegar or sherry with the ginger and water in a pan. Just before the mixture boils, remove from the heat and stir in the *miso*.

3. Pour over the *tofu*. Leave to cool to lukewarm. Just before serving sprinkle with the chopped spring onions.

Aubergine Pizza Slices

———◆———

This is one of my favourite first courses, so to make life easier, I make double and treble quantities of the tomato sauce and freeze it in batches to use whenever I feel like it. I prefer to use Pecorino cheese as it has a strong, piquant flavour. Mozzarella has a lighter, slightly stringy effect.

4 ripe tomatoes, skinned (see page xiii) and sliced plus 150ml (¹/₄ pint) tomato juice, or 1 × 400g (14oz) can of tomatoes
1 teaspoon tomato purée
1 garlic clove, peeled and crushed
fresh or dried thyme leaves
salt and freshly ground black pepper

2 fairly long, thin aubergines cut into 14 cm (5¹/₂ in) thick slices (about 16 slices)
olive oil
125g (4oz) Pecorino or Mozzarella cheese, sliced

1. Mix the tomato and juice, or the contents of the can of tomatoes, with the tomato purée and garlic, and boil until fairly thick. Leave to cool, then flavour with herbs and seasoning.

2. Brush the aubergine slices with olive oil and place under a grill. Leave for 8-10 minutes, turning from time to time.

3. Spread the grilled aubergines with the tomato sauce and cover with slices of cheese. Return to the grill and cook for 2-3 minutes until the cheese bubbles.

Garlic Mushrooms

———◆———

Garlic and mushrooms are the vegetarian equivalent of garlic and snails and this is arguably an even better combination.

425g (1lb) open cup mushrooms, wiped clean
oil for frying
50g (2oz) butter, softened
2 garlic cloves, peeled and crushed
2 tablespoons freshly chopped parsley

pinch dried thyme
salt and freshly ground black pepper
2 teaspoons lemon juice
50g (2oz) fresh breadcrumbs

1. Lightly fry the mushrooms in hot oil for about 20 seconds then drain on kitchen paper. Place in a shallow baking tin, stalks upwards.

2. Mix together the butter, garlic, herbs, seasoning and lemon juice. Spoon some mixture into each mushroom, then lightly press the breadcrumbs on top.

3. Cook under a medium grill for 5 minutes until the breadcrumbs are golden brown.

Stuffed Field Mushrooms
—◆—

There is an eastern feel to this recipe, which uses mushrooms to stuff mushrooms! The large field mushrooms are best cooked in a microwave oven. If you do not have one, bake in a conventional oven for about 15-20 minutes at 200°C/400°F/Gas 6. The secret of this dish lies in careful cooking. Do not overcook the mushrooms or they will shrink too much.

4 large field mushrooms
5 tablespoons olive oil
1 large garlic clove, peeled and
  crushed
salt and freshly ground black
  pepper
175g (6oz) oyster mushrooms,
  sliced

1 tablespoon soy sauce
3 tablespoons dry white wine
the sliced rind of 2 kumquats
a pinch of five-spice powder
1 bunch of fresh chives

1. Place the field mushrooms in a large shallow dish. Mix 4 tablespoons of the oil, the garlic and seasoning and pour over the mushrooms. Cook in the microwave for 3-4 minutes depending on size (or see above). The juices should be running but the mushrooms should still retain some of their bite. Do not overcook or the mushrooms will shrink too much.

2. Heat the remaining oil in a frying pan and sauté the oyster mushrooms for 1 minute. Add the soy sauce, white wine, kumquat rind and the five-spice powder. Bring to the boil and boil fast for a couple of minutes.

3. Arrange sprigs of chives on each plate, place the field mushrooms in the centre and top with oyster mushrooms and juices.

27

Mediterranean Stuffed Aubergines

—◆—

The flavours here depend on the typical Mediterranean ingredients of olive oil, olives and capers. This unusual stuffing can also be used on grilled radiccio.

2 small to medium aubergines, trimmed and halved lengthways
12 pitted black olives, chopped
4 tablespoons pine kernels, very lightly toasted (see page xiii)
4 tablespoons freshly chopped parsley
2 tablespoons raisins
2 garlic cloves, peeled and finely chopped
2 tablespoons drained capers
1 sprig of oregano
olive oil
2 tomatoes, very thinly sliced

1. Preheat the oven to 230°C/450°F/Gas 8.

2. Put the four aubergine halves in a baking dish, cut-side up and slash with a criss-cross pattern.

3. Mix all the remaining ingredients together except for the oil and tomatoes.

4. Spread stuffing mixture over the top of the aubergines, cover with tomato slices and drizzle oil over. Bake for at least an hour.

SNACKS

This section includes a selection of my favourite snack foods. Some take quite a time to prepare but these can be made the day, or even the week, before and stored in the fridge or freezer until the pangs of hunger demand their appearance.

Hummus, Falafel, Italian Rice and Cheese Balls all freeze well. They are good served on their own, with salad or in pitta bread parcels. Spring Rolls and Vegetable Samosas also freeze well.

Some of the dishes in the chapters on buffet food make good snacks and also freeze well. I prepare recipes such as Pâtes de Béziers, Onion and Black Olive Tart, Celeriac and Carrot Flan and Savoury Pumpkin Plait and freeze them in single portions. They are particularly useful for packed lunches, as single portions usually thaw by lunch-time, though if I can remember I do try to take them out of the freezer the night before.

Eggs with Broccoli

This is a very quick way of brightening up scrambled eggs. The soy sauce adds tang to the broccoli.

700g (1¹/₂lb) broccoli or calabrese, *salt and freshly ground black*
   trimmed   *pepper*
6-8 eggs, beaten   2 tablespoons tamari *or soy sauce*
4 tablespoons water

1. Steam the broccoli until just tender. Break up the florets and chop the stems.

2. Mix the eggs with water and seasoning and scramble in the usual way. Pile on to the centre of four warm plates.

3. Toss the broccoli in the *tamari* or soy sauce and spoon round the outside of the egg.

Piperade

— ◆ —

This scrambled egg dish with garlic, peppers and tomatoes comes from the Pays Basque area of southern France. Spain has a very similar dish as well, but there the eggs are set rather than scrambled.

4 red peppers, seeded and
   quartered
3 tablespoons olive oil
1 onion, peeled and sliced
1 garlic clove, peeled and sliced
4 tomatoes, skinned (see page xiii)
   and cut into chunks
1/2 green chilli pepper, seeded and
   chopped

1 bay leaf
a sprig of fresh thyme
6 eggs
2 tablespoons water
salt and freshly ground black
   pepper

1. Grill the peppers until the skiins blister. Place in a soup bowl and cover with a plate. Leave to stand, and then peel and cut into strips.

2. Heat the oil in a heavy pan and fry the onion and garlic until soft. Add the peppers, tomato, chilli, bay leaf and thyme. Cook over a low heat for 30 minutes, stirring occasionally.

3. Beat the eggs and water together and season. Pour into a frying pan. When they start to set, stir in the pepper mixture and continue cooking and stirring until the eggs are lightly scrambled.

Falafel with *Tahina* sauce

—◆—

This Middle-Eastern snack, which has become an Israeli speciality, can be served in pitta bread parcels with a simple salad of lettuce, onions and tomatoes in the base.

1 × 400g (14oz) can of chickpeas, drained
1/2 small onion, peeled and chopped
1 garlic clove, peeled and crushed
1 teaspoon ground cumin
1/2 teaspoon ground coriander
1/2 teaspoon baking powder
a pinch of cayenne
1 tablespoon flour
4 tablespoons freshly chopped parsley
1 tablespoon freshly chopped coriander

salt and freshly ground black pepper
1 egg yolk
water
oil for deep-frying

Tahina sauce
4 tablespoons tahina *paste*
3 tablespoons lemon juice
salt
1 tablespoon cold water

1. Mince the chickpeas or grind in the food processor. Mix in the onion, garlic, ground spices, baking powder and cayenne. Next add the flour, fresh herbs and seasoning. Finally bind with the egg yolk. (You may need a little water as well.)

2. Shape into walnut-sized balls. Deep-fry in cooking oil. Drain on absorbent paper.

3. To make the sauce, mix the *tahina* and lemon juice in a blender or food processor, adding a little salt and only enough water to give a light consistency – maybe a little thicker than single cream or like runny double cream.

4. Serve the balls on a plate with some sauce, or in pitta breads with salad and a little sauce on top.

31

Italian Crunchy Cheese Balls

—◆—

You need to use Italian risotto rice for this recipe. It is rather stickier than long grain rice and helps to hold the balls together. After stage 1 of the method the mixture can be held in the fridge or freezer and cooked when required. Allow more time for cooking from frozen.

The balls are soft on the inside, crisp on the outside. Serve them with salad or coleslaw, or simply eat with your fingers.

MAKES 16

175g (6oz) Italian risotto rice
salt and freshly ground black
*   pepper*
1 egg, beaten
175g (6oz) well flavoured cheese

1 teaspoon dried oregano
1 teaspoon tomato purée
50g (2oz) dried breadcrumbs
oil for deep-frying

1. Cook the rice in plenty of salted water for 10-12 minutes until only just tender. Drain very well and mix with all the remaining ingredients except the breadcrumbs and oil.

2. Place in the fridge for a couple of hours to chill.

3. Shape the mixture into balls, roll in breadcrumbs and deep-fry for about 2-3 minutes. Drain well on absorbent paper.

Indian Toast

—◆—

An Indian version of cheese on toast! For an even more substantial snack, crown the spicy topping with a poached egg.

125g (4oz) Cheddar cheese, grated
2 tablespoons mango chutney
1 teaspoon curry powder

4 large slices of bread
4 tomatoes, sliced

1. Mix cheese, chutney and curry powder to a thick paste.

2. Grill the bread on both sides. Cover with tomato slices and top with the cheese mixture.

3. Place under the grill for 3-4 minutes until the cheese is bubbly.

Italian Bruschetta

—◆—

This Italian dish has become very popular beyond the shores of the Mediterranean. It was originally served as an appetiser, but makes a delicious quickly prepared snack. Use *ciabatta* – flat Italian bread loaves – or fresh sticks of French bread.

1 large flat Italian bread loaf, or 2
*   short French sticks*
2 garlic cloves, peeled
75ml (3fl oz) olive oil
4-5 sprigs of basil

6 tomatoes, sliced
salt and freshly ground black
*   pepper*
grated Parmesan cheese (optional)

1. Slice the loaf or French sticks in half lengthways and open up. Cut the Italian loaf into two. Rub all over with the garlic cloves, leaving bits of garlic behind. Then brush all over with olive oil.

2. Bake in a hot oven, at 230°C/450°F/Gas 8 for 8-10 minutes, or toast under the grill for 4-5 minutes each side. Dot with sprigs of basil and arrange slices of tomato over the top.

3. Season and place under the grill for a further minute or two. Add Parmesan if liked.

Popovers

—◆—

These American wholemeal puffs are quick to make, and are delicious served with maple syrup. Try them for breakfast.

a little butter or oil
4 eggs, separated
600ml (1 pint) milk

5 tablespoons wholemeal flour
1 teaspoon salt

1. Preheat the oven to 230°C/450°F/Gas 8, and grease some muffin tins.

2. Beat the egg yolks until they are stiff and pale yellow in colour. Add the milk and flour alternately, beating all the time.

3. Add the salt to the egg whites and whisk until they are very stiff indeed. Stir a tablespoon of the whites into the yolk mixture and then carefully fold in the rest.

4. Spoon into the greased muffin tins and bake for 30 minutes. Serve straight from the oven.

Hummus

—◆—

Serve as a dip, as they do in Greek and Cypriot restaurants, in sandwiches or as a snack or starter with olive oil, pitta bread and raw vegetables.

1 × 430g (1lb) can of chickpeas,
  drained
2 tablespoons tahina *paste*
1-2 garlic cloves, peeled and
  crushed
juice of 1 lemon
salt

Garnish
2-3 tablespoons olive oil
ground cumin
paprika
sprigs of continental parsley

1. Rub the chickpeas through a sieve or blend in a food processor. Add all the remaining ingredients and blend well together.

2. Spoon into a bowl, pour on olive oil and garnish with the spices and herbs.

Open Sandwiches
—◆—

Danish open sandwiches are much more attractive to look at than traditional closed ones, yet they are very quick to make. The secret is due to at least two major ingredients with a garnish. Try to get some height into the topping by arranging over lettuce leaves or by heaping up small spoonfuls of chopped ingredients.

The Base

Any kind of firm, fairly thickly cut bread can be used, but the Danes choose rye bread. Butter liberally – this is what keeps the topping in place.

Toppings

1. Chopped egg and onion (see page 164) on a bed of watercress with sliced tomatoes and capers.

2. Sliced beetroot on lettuce with orange segments and horseradish sauce; garnish with parsley.

3. Grated Cheddar cheese and carrot piled over alfalfa or cress with sliced cucumber and fresh tarragon.

4. Sliced avocado with cranberry jelly and cottage cheese.

5. Sliced blue cheese with halved green and black grapes and sliced celery over lettuce.

6. Sliced mushrooms with walnut halves and lambs lettuce, on mayonnaise.

7. Hummus (see page 34) with black olives and sliced tomatoes on lettuce with freshly chopped mixed herbs.

8. Watercress with apple slices on peanut butter.

Savoury Muffins
—◆—

It is simplicity itself to rustle up these moist and flavoursome American-style muffins. Serve warm. If there are any left over, store in an airtight tin and reheat gently before serving. Nibble at them any time you like!

MAKES 12

a little cooking oil
300g (10oz) wholemeal flour
4 level teaspoons baking powder
¹/₂ teaspoon salt
2 large eggs
250ml (8fl oz) milk
50g (2oz) butter or margarine, melted
125g (4oz) carrots, peeled and coarsely grated

25g (1oz) sunflower seeds

Flavouring 1
50g (2oz) Cheddar cheese, grated
4-6 spring onions chopped

Flavouring 2
50g (2oz) canned sweetcorn with peppers, drained
6 stuffed olives, chopped

1. Preheat the oven to 190°C/375°F/Gas 5 and grease twelve muffin or deep bun pans.

2. Mix the flour, baking powder and salt in a bowl.

3. Whisk the eggs with the milk and melted butter, and pour over the dry ingredients. Mix together and add the carrots, sunflower seeds and your chosen flavouring.

4. Spoon into the prepared tins. Do not fill too full. Bake for 45-50 minutes until springy to the touch. Leave to cool a little before serving.

Fried Halloumi Cheese with Capers
—◆—

A Greek restaurant near my home serves this tasty dish as a starter, but it occurred to me that it could make a good snack meal with plenty of crusty bread.

4 thick slices of Halloumi cheese
shredded iceberg lettuce
1/2 small onion, peeled and cut into
 rings

tomato and lemon wedges
6 tablespoons warm olive oil
4 tablespoons drained capers
freshly ground black pepper

1. Place the cheese under a hot grill to cook on both sides until lightly browned.

2. Have ready four serving plates each with a small mound of shredded lettuce topped with onion rings.

3. Place a piece of grilled cheese on each one. Arrange tomato and lemon wedges at the side. Pour the oil over all and sprinkle with capers and black pepper.

Onion Bread

This unusual bread comes from Syria. Try it warm with hard-boiled eggs, black olives and salad.

MAKES 1 loaf

1 small onion, peeled and finely
 chopped
3 tablespoons olive oil
225g (8oz) self-raising flour

1/2 teaspoon salt
1 teaspoon baking powder
1/2 teaspoon dried thyme
milk

1. Gently fry the onion in the olive oil until it turns transparent.

2. Sift the flour, salt and baking powder into a bowl. Add the thyme and mix well with a spoon. Make a well in the centre and add the fried onions and sufficient water to make a fairly soft dough.

3. Turn out on to a floured surface and knead for about 10 minutes until the dough is elastic and no longer sticks to your hands. Place in a 450g (1lb) loaf tin and leave to rest in a warm place for a while.

4. Preheat the oven to 180°C/350°F/Gas 4.

5. Brush the top of the loaf with milk. Bake for about 1 hour and 20-25 minutes until golden on top and a skewer inserted into the centre comes out clean. Remove from the tin and leave to cool on a wire rack.

Jacket Potatoes
—◆—

Jacket potatoes can be left to cook themselves in the oven – at 200°C/400°F/Gas 6 for about an hour – or, if you do not mind limp skins, they can be cooked very quickly in the microwave. A combination of both methods works well. If time is really short most of these toppings are also very good on toast!

The potato stuffing recipes given here are sufficient for four large jackets, so divide by four if you are on your own.

1. Leeks with Caraway

50g (2oz) butter
700g (1¹/₂lb) leeks, trimmed and
  sliced

¹/₄ teaspoon caraway seeds
salt and freshly ground black
  pepper

1. Melt the butter in a large pan and gently sauté the leeks until they begin to soften. Mix in the caraway seeds and seasoning.

2. Spoon on to the split potatoes.

2. Spicy Onion and Carrot

450g (1lb) onions, peeled and
  sliced
2 tablespoons cooking oil
225g (8oz) carrots, peeled and
  grated

2 tablespoons sultanas
1 tablespoon tomato purée
1-2 tablespoons soy sauce
freshly ground black pepper

1. Fry the onion in oil to soften. Toss in the carrots and sultanas and stir-fry for 1 minute.

2. Mix together the tomato purée, soy sauce and pepper and add to the vegetables. Toss again to mix and heat through.

3. Spoon on to the split potatoes.

3. Blue Cheese and Walnuts

225g (8oz) blue cheese (Roquefort,
  Stilton or Gorgonzola)
50g (2oz) walnut halves, coarsely
  chopped

1-2 tablespoons plain yoghurt or
  fromage frais

1. Dice the cheese and mix with the remaining ingredients.

2. Spoon on to the split potatoes.

4. Mushroom and Garlic

50g (2oz) fresh wild mushrooms,
  or 15g (1/20z) dried ceps, porcini
  or morels
3 tablespoons olive oil
2-3 garlic cloves, peeled and
  chopped
350g (12oz) button or cup
  mushrooms, sliced

125g (4oz) oyster mushrooms,
  sliced
salt and freshly ground black
  pepper
4 tablespoons freshly chopped
  parsley

1. Slice the fresh mushrooms, or soak the dried ones in a little boiling water, and slice after 15 minutes. Retain the soaking liquid to use in this and other recipes.

2. Heat the oil in a frying pan and fry the garlic. Add all the mushrooms and toss over the heat for 2-3 minutes to soften them, adding a little mushroom liquid or water towards the end.

3. Season, spoon on to the split potatoes, and serve sprinkled with freshly chopped parsley.

5. Herby *Tahina*

4 tablespoons tahina
150ml (1/4 pint) water
freshly ground black pepper

6 tablespoons freshly chopped
  mixed herbs (chives, parsley,
  basil, tarragon or chervil)

1. Mix the *tahina* to a smooth cream with the water and stir in the pepper and herbs.

2. Spoon on to the split potatoes.

Spring Rolls

—◆—

All twelve of these Chinese delicacies will probably vanish just as quickly as you can make them. But they can be frozen very successfully after half the cooking time. To serve later, deep-fry directly from the freezer.

MAKES 12

12 spring roll wrappers
1 egg, beaten
oil for deep-frying

Filling
1 tablespoon cooking oil
1 onion, peeled and sliced
2.5 cm (1 in) fresh root ginger, peeled and chopped
1 garlic clove, peeled and crushed
1 carrot, peeled and cut into thin sticks

75g (3oz) mushrooms, sliced
1 red pepper, seeded and thinly sliced
75g (3oz) beansprouts
75g (3oz) bamboo shoots, cut into sticks
1 teaspoon cornflour
salt and freshly ground black pepper
1 teaspoon soy sauce

1. For the filling, heat the oil in a wok or frying pan and stir-fry the onion, ginger, garlic and carrot sticks for 2 minutes. Add the mushrooms and pepper, and continue cooking for another 2 minutes. Toss in the beansprouts and bamboo shoots.

2. Quickly mix together all the remaining ingredients and pour into the pan, stirring all the time.

3. Place spoonfuls of the mixture in the centre of each spring roll wrapper. Roll up and fold in the ends. Seal with beaten egg and secure with a cocktail stick.

4. Deep-fry for about 3 minutes until crisp and golden. Drain and serve.

Vegetable Samosas

—◆—

These little Indian snacks can be made with almost any kind of vegetables. Store in the fridge or freezer and cook as required, allowing more time when cooking from frozen.

MAKES 8

oil for deep-frying, if used

Filling
1 onion, peeled and finely chopped
1 garlic clove, peeled and chopped
1 tablespoon cooking oil
1 tablespoon each garam masala or
   curry powder, and ground cumin
1 teaspoon ground coriander
salt and freshly ground black
   pepper
4 tablespoons vegetable stock (see
   page xii)

450g (1lb) potatoes, peeled and
   diced
175g (6oz) peas
2 carrots, peeled and diced

Pastry
125g (4oz) plain flour
a pinch of salt
1 teaspoon bicarbonate of soda
15g ($^1/_2$oz) butter, melted
3-3$^1/_2$ teaspoons water

1. Start by making the filling. Fry the onion and garlic in the oil for 3-4 minutes. Stir in the spices, seasoning and stock. Add all the remaining ingredients and simmer for 20 minutes until the vegetables are cooked and all the liquid has evaporated.

2. To make the pastry, sift the flour, salt and bicarbonate of soda into a bowl. Stir in the melted butter and water and knead to an elastic dough.

3. Divide into eight pieces and roll out each one to make a 10 cm (4 in) square. Place a tablespoon of filling on each square and fold over to form a triangle. Dampen the edges of the pastry and pinch well together.

4. Deep-fry in hot oil for about 3-4 minutes until golden and slightly bubbly, or bake in an oven preheated to 220°C/425°F/Gas 7 for 20-30 minutes.

The Main Course

PASTA DISHES

Pasta is an easy way of increasing the amount of cereals we eat, and wholemeal pasta also offers plenty of fibre.

Pasta is so quick and simple to prepare that it features on my dinner table quite frequently. It's fun to make two toppings if I have the time, but one will do.

The quantities given here are for main-course dishes. Smaller amounts make good starters and larger quantities can be served as the centrepiece of a hot buffet. Many of the stir-fry dishes in this book can also be served with pasta.

Rigatoni with Goat's Cheese and Parsley

This dish could hardly be easier to make but the flavours – of the goat's cheese, parsley and olive oil – are much more complex than you might expect. I use a hard goat's cheese from Somerset but any goat's cheese can be used. Crumble or chop softer cheeses.

350g (12oz) rigatoni (fat tubes)
salt
1 teaspoon olive oil
175g (6oz) hard goat's cheese, grated
2 tablespoons extra virgin olive oil
4 tablespoons freshly chopped parsley
a pinch of dried oregano
freshly ground black pepper

1. Cook the rigatoni as directed on the pack in plenty of salted boiling water with a little oil.

2. When the pasta is just cooked *al dente,* drain and toss with all the remaining ingredients. Serve at once.

Pasta Ribbons with Sautéed Spring Vegetables
—◆—

This is best made in the early summer when the new vegetables are coming into the shops. At other times of the year vary the vegetables to suit what's available. It makes an unusual starter, but the quantities can be increased and the recipe served as a supper dish.

225g (8oz) pasta ribbons
salt
2 tablespoons olive oil
2-3 spring onions, finely chopped
2-3 new carrots, scrubbed and cut into sticks, or large carrots, scrubbed and shredded into ribbons
175g (6oz) mangetout, topped and tailed

50g (2oz) peas or broccoli sprigs
1 tablespoon freshly chopped parsley
4 tablespoons grated Parmesan cheese
freshly ground black pepper
2 tablespoons pine kernels, toasted (see page xiii)

1. Cook pasta ribbons in plenty of salted boiling water together with a teaspoon of the olive oil, following the instructions on the pack. Drain and toss in a little more olive oil. Keep warm.

2. Heat the remaining olive oil in a pan and sauté the spring onion and carrot sticks for 3-4 minutes. Add the mangetout and peas or broccoli sprigs and continue cooking for a further 4-5 minutes until all the vegetables are tender but still slightly crisp.

3. Spoon over the pasta and top with chopped parsley, Parmesan, pine kernels and black pepper.

Fusilli with Fresh Tomato and Basil Sauce

—◆—

Sadly the tomatoes we buy in northern Europe are not usually as ripe and flavoursome as those from the Mediterranean. So I generally cheat a little and add some tomato purée. The carrot also adds a certain sweetness.

1 small onion, peeled and finely chopped
1-3 garlic cloves, to taste, peeled and crushed
just over 1 tablespoon olive oil
1 large carrot, peeled and grated
1kg (2lb) ripe tomatoes, skinned (see page xiii) and chopped

1 tablespoon tomato purée
salt and freshly ground black pepper
a good handful of fresh basil
350g (12oz) fusilli (spirals)

1. Fry the onion and garlic in the oil (leaving 1 teaspoon for the pasta) until lightly browned. Add the carrot and cook for a further minute. Add the tomatoes, tomato purée and seasoning. Simmer over a low heat for 10 minutes. Rub through a sieve and return to the heat.

2. Cook the fusilli as directed on the pack in salted water with a little oil until *al dente*. Drain.

3. Tear the basil into small pieces and add to the sauce just before pouring it over the drained pasta.

Vermicelli D'Abruzzo

—◆—

This is a popular topping for pasta in the Adriatic province of Abruzzo, where it is served with the thick tubular local pasta. However, I think it is more fun to mix the strips of peppers with vermicelli (thin spaghetti).

350g (12oz) vermicelli
1 teaspoon olive oil
4-5 peppers, mixed red, green and yellow

3 tablespoons extra virgin olive oil
2 tablespoons capers, well rinsed
freshly ground black pepper
grated Parmesan cheese (optional)

46

1. Cook the pasta as directed on the pack in salted boiling water with a teaspoonful of olive oil.

2. Cut the peppers into quarters and remove the seeds. Place skin up under a hot grill and leave until the skin is blackened. Place in a bowl and cover with a lid. Peel off and discard the skin after about 15-20 minutes. Cut the flesh into long thin strips.

3. Drain the pasta well and toss with the strips of pepper and extra virgin olive oil. Serve sprinkled with capers, black pepper and Parmesan, if liked.

Farfalle with Boursin and Walnut Sauce
—◆—

This is one of the quickest pasta sauces I know, with lots of flavour and texture. I like to serve it with bows as the sauce seems to collect in delicious quantities in the folds of the pasta.

350g (12oz) farfalle (pasta bows)
salt
1 teaspoon olive oil
2 × 150g (5oz) Boursin cheese
125ml (4fl oz) single cream

12-14 walnut halves, cut into quarters
4 tablespoons freshly chopped parsley

1. Cook the pasta as directed on the pack in plenty of salted boiling water with a teaspoonful of oil.

2. Cut the Boursin into chunks and place in a small saucepan with the cream. Heat gently, stirring all the time to produce a smooth creamy sauce.

3. Drain the pasta and toss with the Boursin sauce and walnuts. Serve sprinkled with freshly chopped parsley.

Spaghetti with Wild Mushrooms

—◆—

I always keep a supply of dried Italian or French mushrooms in my store cupboard. They are expensive, but a very small amount will give a wonderfully strong flavour. Use them on their own for special occasions or mix with button mushrooms for everyday use.

Do try to find the sun-dried tomato paste as it adds such an inimitable flavour.

25g (1oz) dried ceps
2 heaped tablespoons tomato purée
2 heaped teaspoons sun-dried
* tomato paste*
1 onion, peeled and finely chopped
2 garlic cloves, peeled and crushed

just over 1 tablespoon olive oil
salt and freshly ground black
* pepper*
350g (12oz) spaghetti
salt

1. Place the dried mushrooms in a bowl and just cover with boiling water. Leave to stand for half an hour. Drain and chop, reserving the liquid to mix with the two tomato pastes.

2. Fry the onion and garlic in 1 tablespoon of the oil until golden. Add the mushrooms and tomato mixture and seasoning. Bring the mixture to the boil and simmer until the right consistency is achieved.

3. In the meantime cook the pasta as directed on the pack in plenty of salted boiling water with a little oil. Drain well.

4. Serve the pasta in bowls with the sauce spooned over.

Tagliatelle with Pesto Sauce and Black Olives

—◆—

The black olives seem to add an extra dimension to the classic Ligurian 'pasta with pesto' combination. The effect is somehow lighter and less oily, and I find I can eat much more of it. It is, however, essential to use fresh basil.

350g (12oz) tagliatelle
12-14 black olives, stoned and cut
   in half

Pesto Sauce
50g (2oz) fresh basil leaves
2 garlic cloves, peeled

2 tablespoons pine kernels
salt
25g (1oz) Parmesan cheese, finely
   grated
50-75ml (2-3 fl oz) olive oil

1. Start by making the pesto sauce. Very finely chop the basil leaves, garlic and pine kernels, or grind in a mortar. Add a pinch of salt and the cheese, and then stir in most of the oil, a little at a time. If possible finish off in a blender.

2. Cook the tagliatelle in plenty of salted boiling water with a teaspoon of olive oil. When the pasta is just cooked, drain.

3. Toss pasta in the pesto sauce. Spoon on to individual plates and top with the halved olives.

Marrow with Macaroni
—◆—

Marrow makes a really juicy accompaniment to macaroni which can sometimes be rather dry. This quantity makes a good first course.

1 onion, peeled and thinly sliced
2 tablespoons olive oil
a knob of butter
1 small vegetable marrow, peeled
   and seeded
1 tablespoon freshly chopped basil

1 tablespoon tomato purée
salt and freshly ground black
   pepper
175g (6oz) quick-cook short
   macaroni

1. Fry the onion in half the olive oil and the butter until very lightly browned.

2. Cut the marrow into small dice and add to the pan. Continue cooking over a low heat, stirring from time to time until the marrow just begins to soften. This will take about 8 minutes depending on the size of the dice. Stir in the basil and tomato purée and season to taste.

3. Meanwhile cook the macaroni as directed on the pack. Drain very well and then sauté in the remaining oil. Add the marrow mixture and toss well together. Serve sprinkled with freshly ground black pepper.

Spaghetti with Walnut, Parsley and Basil Sauce

———◆———

This is another simple variation on a classic pesto sauce and has an excellent flavour of its own. Serve with grated Parmesan or Wellington Cheddar cheese.

50g (2oz) shelled walnuts, coarsely ground
1 large garlic clove, peeled and chopped
a generous handful of parsley, freshly chopped
5 tablespoons virgin olive oil
2 tablespoons very hot water
10-14 fresh basil leaves
225g (8oz) spaghetti
salt and freshly ground black pepper

1. Gently heat 2 tablespoons of the olive oil in a pan, then add the garlic and the parsley. Stir over the low heat. Add the nuts and cook for a minute or so but do not allow to brown. Stir in the remaining olive oil and the water. Season and remove from the heat.

2. Cut the basil leaves thinly, stir them into the sauce and leave in the pan on one side.

3. Cook the spaghetti as directed on the pack in salted boiling water with a little oil. Cook until it is just tender. Drain, and mix in the sauce.

opposite: Spaghetti with Walnut, Parsley and Basil Sauce (above)

Spaghetti with Onions and Sun-Dried Tomatoes

————◆————

The combination of the piquancy of the sun-dried tomatoes and the sweetness of the onions is very unusual.

I do not think it can be stressed too often how important it is to use freshly grated Parmesan cheese. This cheese keeps well in the fridge. Take out and grate about an hour before it will be required (all cheeses should be served at room temperature).

350g (12oz) spaghetti
salt
2 tablespoons olive oil
25g (1oz) sun-dried tomatoes

2-3 onions, peeled and sliced
freshly ground black pepper
freshly grated Parmesan cheese

1. Cook the spaghetti in lightly salted boiling water with 1 teaspoon of the oil. Follow the cooking instructions on the pack and start tasting to see if the pasta is ready 2-3 minutes before the end of the cooking time.

2. Place tomatoes in a bowl, just cover with boiling water and leave to stand for 10-15 minutes.

3. Heat the remaining oil in a small frying pan and fry the onions until they start to brown.

4. Drain the tomatoes and cut into strips. Toss with the onions.

5. Drain the pasta and spoon the onion and tomato over the top. Serve with freshly grated Parmesan.

opposite: Garlic Mushrooms (pages 26-7)

Tagliatelle with Cannellini Beans

—◆—

This recipe is very similar to the *Fettucini al Stufo* which is a speciality of La Spezia, an Italian port on the Mediterranean. The combination of pasta and beans makes a substantial winter dish. Serve with a tossed green salad.

1¹/₂ *tablespoons olive oil*
2 garlic cloves, peeled and chopped
1 onion, peeled and chopped
3 tablespoons freshly chopped
  parsley
a little fresh rosemary
125ml (4ft oz) red wine

1 × 400g (14oz) can of tomatoes
salt and freshly ground black
  pepper
1 × 400g (14oz) can of cannellini
  beans, drained
350g (12oz) tagliatelle

1. Heat a tablespoon of the oil in a pan and gently fry the garlic and onion for 2-3 minutes. Add the herbs and cook for a further minute. Pour on the wine and turn up the heat. Boil until half the mixture has evaporated.

2. Add the tomatoes and seasoning and cook for 15 minutes or until the sauce is quite thick.

3. Add the beans and cook for a further 5 minutes.

4. Cook the spaghetti as directed on the pack in plenty of salted boiling water with a little oil. Drain well.

5. Serve the pasta with the bean sauce spooned over the top.

Pasticcio

——◆——

There are both Italian and Greek versions of this macaroni and aubergine pie, but every family there seems to have its own special way of making it. This is a very good dish to serve at a buffet party.

SERVES 8-10

2 large aubergines, sliced
salt
225g (8oz) macaroni
1 teaspoon olive oil
1 × 400g (14oz) can of tomatoes
1 garlic clove, peeled and crushed
1 tablespoon tomato purée

2 tablespoons freshly chopped basil
freshly ground black pepper
25g (1oz) butter
25g (1oz) flour
250ml (8fl oz) milk
1 egg, beaten

1. Sprinkle the aubergines with salt and leave to stand in a colander over a plate until required, but for at least 30 minutes. Rinse well and squeeze dry.

2. Cook the macaroni as directed on the pack in plenty of salted boiling water with the oil. Drain.

3. Empty the contents of the can of tomatoes into a pan and add the garlic, tomato purée, basil, salt and pepper and bring to the boil. Cook for 10-15 minutes until fairly thick. Rub through a sieve or purée in a blender. Mix with the drained pasta.

4. Pre-heat the oven to 200°C/400°F/Gas 6.

5. Arrange half the aubergine slices in the base of a greased pie dish and cover with half the pasta. Add another layer of aubergines and another layer of pasta, finishing them both.

6. Place the butter, flour and milk in a pan and bring to the boil, stirring with a wire whisk. When the mixture thickens remove from the heat and beat in the egg. Pour over the pie and bake for 40 minutes.

Penne with Zucchini

——◆——

This courgette and pasta dish is just as good served chilled as it is hot. I like to serve it hot as a first course or chilled on a cold buffet. Fresh basil is essential to the flavour; buy it growing in a pot and keep in the kitchen ready for instant flavouring and garnish.

450g (1lb) courgettes, trimmed and sliced
4½ tablespoons olive oil
salt and freshly ground black pepper
75ml (3 fl oz) cow's or goat's milk yoghurt
1 teaspoon corn or rice flour
225g (8oz) penne (quills)
2 tablespoons chopped basil
some whole basil leaves for garnish

1. Fry the courgettes in 4 tablespoons of the oil until very lightly browned. Place in a blender with the seasoning, yoghurt and flour, and purée. Return to a saucepan and place over a gentle heat to thicken. Stir from time to time.

2. Cook the penne as directed on the pack with plenty of salted boiling water and a little oil. Drain well and spoon into a dish.

3. Stir the basil into the sauce and pour over the top of the pasta. Garnish with the whole basil leaves.

Sicilian Pasta

—◆—

This delicious aubergine and mushroom sauce is popular in Sicily, and can be served with any kind of pasta shapes. Marsala, a fortified dessert wine from Sicily, is similar to *Oloroso* sherry or Madeira, and adds an interesting flavour.

1 onion, peeled and finely chopped
5 tablespoons olive oil
1 aubergine, diced
1 garlic clove, peeled and crushed
4 tablespoons freshly chopped
*   parsley*

1 tablespoon freshly chopped basil
225g (8oz) mushrooms, sliced
50ml (2fl oz) Marsala
salt and freshly ground black
*   pepper*
350g (12oz) pasta

1. Fry the onion in half the oil for 2-3 minutes. Add the aubergine and continue cooking for 8-10 minutes until the aubergine is tender and lightly browned.

2. In another pan fry the garlic and herbs in the remaining oil for 1 minute and then add the mushrooms. Fry gently for 4-5 minutes and then add the Marsala and seasoning. Increase the heat and boil until most of the liquid has evaporated.

3. Add the onion and aubergine to the mushroom mixture and simmer together for a further minute or so.

4. Cook the pasta until *al dente* in plenty of salted boiling water and a little oil. Drain and serve with the sauce.

Lasagne Rolls with Tomato Sauce

———◆———

This unusual way with Italian lasagne – rolling it into catherine wheels – looks very effective. Serve with freshly grated Parmesan cheese.

8 long narrow pieces of ordinary or
   quick-cook lasagne
salt
1 teaspoon cooking oil
1.5kg (3lb) fresh spinach, cooked
   and chopped or 1 × 450g (1lb)
   pack of frozen chopped spinach,
   thawed
350g (12oz) Ricotta cheese
150g (5oz) quark or fromage frais

salt and freshly ground black
   pepper
freshly grated Parmesan cheese

Tomato sauce
1 × 225g (8oz) can of tomatoes
   with their juice
600ml (1 pint) tomato juice
1/4 teaspoon dried thyme

1. If not using quick-cook lasagne, cook the lasagne in lightly salted boiling water with a teaspoon of cooking oil for about 12 minutes or as directed on the pack. Drain and lay out on a piece of oiled greaseproof or Bakewell paper. Plunge quick-cook pasta into boiling water to soften and remove at once. Cut lasagne in half lengthways.

2. Preheat the oven to 200°C/400°F/Gas 6.

3. Squeeze out all the liquid from the spinach and mix with the cheeses and the seasoning. Spread the mixture all along the length of each piece of lasagne and roll each one up like a catherine wheel. Place in a heatproof dish.

4. For the sauce, purée the contents of the can of tomatoes in a blender or processor, or rub through a sieve. Mix with the tomato juice, thyme and some salt and pepper.

5. Pour into the dish with the lasagne and cover with foil. Bake for about 15 minutes. To serve, sprinkle with a little freshly grated Parmesan cheese.

RICE AND CEREAL DISHES

The cooking times for rice in this section are based on white rice or the specially treated semi-cooked brown rice. If you use the untreated, fibre-rich nutty brown rice available at health-food shops you will need to extend the cooking time from 12-15 minutes to 20-25 minutes. All the recipes use long-grain rice unless risotto rice is specified. The latter should be arborio rice from Italy.

Some of the rice dishes, such as Singapore Rice, Afghan Rice and Oriental Rice Pilaf, are very good served on their own with a yoghurt-based salad such as Raita (see page 169), or simple stir-fry vegetables. Other recipes in this chapter go well with a mixture of dishes. The risottos, too, are very good served on their own with a tossed green salad. Couscous is a meal in itself.

Savoury Baked Rice

This dish has lots of texture, flavour and colour, and goes particularly well with all kinds of oriental food.

125g (4oz) basmati rice
2 leeks, trimmed and very finely
   chopped
1 courgette, trimmed and very
   finely chopped
4 tablespoons frozen peas
3 tablespoons mixed salted nuts,
   chopped

2 tablespoons chopped apricots or
   raisins
salt and freshly ground black
   pepper
250ml (8fl oz) boiling water

1. Preheat the oven to 190°C/375°F/Gas 5.

2. Mix all the ingredients together and place in a casserole dish. Bake for 45 minutes, until all the liquid has been absorbed.

3. Leave to stand for 5 minutes and fluff up before serving.

Singapore Rice

—◆—

The coconut and curry powder contribute to the aromatic flavour of this Malaysian rice dish. Serve with any of the dishes in the stir-fry section (see pages 72-83), or as part of a hot buffet.

SERVES 6-8

1 onion, peeled and finely chopped
1 small green pepper, seeded and
* finely chopped*
2 tablespoons cooking oil
1/2 teaspoon mild curry powder
75g (3oz) creamed coconut
1 × 225g (8oz) can of pineapple
* slices, drained and chopped*

2 tablespoons toasted flaked
* almonds*
2 tablespoons sultanas or raisins
350g (12oz) long-grain rice
700ml (24fl oz) vegetable stock (see
* page xii)*
springs of fresh coriander

1. Gently stir-fry the onion and green pepper in the oil in a saucepan. Cook for 2 minutes and then add all the remaining ingredients except the fresh coriander.

2. Bring to the boil. Stir once and cover with a lid. Reduce the heat and cook for 15 minutes until all the water has been absorbed.

3. Turn off the heat and leave to stand for 5 minutes before serving. Garnish with sprigs of fresh coriander.

Caribbean Rice

——◆——

The mixed cultural backgrounds of the Caribbean – African, Chinese and Indian – have all contributed to the flavour of this dish. Try to use limes, as the flavour really is quite different to lemons. The dish can be eaten on its own, but it is also very useful on a hot buffet table.

1 garlic clove, peeled and finely chopped
1 onion, peeled and finely chopped
1 tablespoon cooking oil
225g (8oz) long-grain rice
50g (2oz) raisins
450ml (³/₄ pint) strong vegetable stock (see page xii)
1 tablespoon soy sauce
1 tablespoon oriental sesame oil

1 teaspoon ground turmeric
1 teaspoon minced lime peel
2 tablespoons pine kernels, toasted (see page xiii)
¹/₄ green pepper, seeded and cut into short strips

Garnish
sliced lime rind
fresh coriander leaves

1. Fry the garlic and onion in the cooking oil in a large pan for 2 minutes until they turn transparent.

2. Add the rice, stir, then add the raisins, stock, soy sauce, sesame oil, turmeric and minced peel. Bring to the boil, stir and cover. Reduce the heat and cook for a further 15 minutes until all the liquid has been absorbed.

3. Leave to stand for 5 minutes and then stir in the remaining ingredients, retaining a third to sprinkle on the top. Garnish with sliced lime rind and fresh coriander and serve at once.

Curried Rice and Peas

——◆——

Rice and peas is a combination which turns up in countries as diverse as Italy and Jamaica, Brazil and India. Sometimes the 'peas' really are peas, at other times they are beans. So make up your own recipe by choosing different pulses and flavourings.

1 teaspoon whole cumin seeds
6 black peppercorns
seeds from 3 cardamom pods
2 tablespoons cooking oil
1 onion, peeled and chopped
1 garlic clove, peeled and chopped
1 teaspoon garam masala *or curry powder*

225g (8oz) long-grain rice
475ml (16fl oz) water
225g (8oz) cooked peas or canned beans, drained
salt and freshly ground black pepper

1. Fry the whole seeds in hot oil for about a minute. Add the onion and garlic and continue cooking for a further 4-5 minutes, browning the onions slightly.

2. Stir in the curry powder and rice, making sure that the rice is well coated with oil and spices. Pour on the water, and bring to the boil. Stir once and cover with a lid. Simmer for 12 minutes.

3. Stir in the peas or beans and seasoning, and cook for a further minute or so until all the liquid has been taken up. Leave to stand for 3-5 minutes before serving.

Aubergine Pilau

——◆——

This interestingly spiced dish comes from Saudi Arabia. It is excellent served with vegetable kebabs or satay and salad.

¹/₄ teaspoon whole mustard seeds
  or cumin seeds
¹/₂ teaspoon poppy seeds
2 whole cloves
¹/₂ teaspoon ground turmeric
¹/₄ teaspoon ground cinnamon
1 tablespoon ground almonds

50g (2oz) butter, or 1 tablespoon
  oil and 25g (1oz) butter
1 aubergine, peeled and sliced
1 onion, peeled and finely chopped
225g (8oz) long-grain rice
450ml (³/₄ pint) water
salt

1. Fry the spices and ground almonds in the butter or a mixture of butter and oil. After a minute or so add the diced aubergine and stir well. Next add the onion and continue to fry gently for about 5 minutes, stirring regularly.

2. Add the rice and stir well to make sure it is well mixed in. Pour on the water, and season. Bring to the boil and reduce the heat. Cover and simmer for 15 minutes until the rice is tender and all the liquid has been absorbed.

3. Turn off the heat and leave for 5 minutes. Fluff up the rice with a fork before serving.

Afghan Rice

—◆—

This is a really well flavoured rice dish which is very good eaten on its own with Raita (see page 169) and salad. The combination of the curry powder and the cinnamon reveal influences of both the Far East and the Middle East.

3 tablespoons pine kernels
1 onion, peeled and finely chopped
2 tablespoons cooking oil
225g (8oz) long-grain rice
475ml (16fl oz) strong vegetable
  stock (see page xii)

1 small phial or packet of saffron
2 tablespoons raisins
a pinch of mild curry powder
1 cinnamon stick

1. Toast the pine kernels under a hot grill to brown them all over. Keep on one side.

2. Fry the onion in the oil until lightly browned. This will take about 5-6 minutes.

3. Add the rice and stir to coat the grains well with oil. Add the stock and all the remaining ingredients. Bring the mixture to the boil. Stir once and cover with a lid. Reduce the heat and simmer for 15 minutes until all the liquid has been taken up and the rice is cooked through.

4. Turn off the heat and leave to stand for 3-4 minutes before fluffing up and serving.

Texan Rice

—◆—

This recipe comes from a Texan friend who actually refers to it as Mexican Rice! However, the genuine Mexican version is probably rather hotter than this mild but delicious dish.

2 tablespoons cooking oil
1 green chilli, seeded and finely
  chopped
a pinch of saffron
225g (8oz) long-grain rice
1 × 400g (14oz) can of tomatoes
150ml (¹/₄ pint) water
2 Spanish onions, peeled and cut
  into rings

1 red pepper, seeded and cut into
  rings
1 green pepper, seeded and cut into
  rings
salt and freshly ground black
  pepper

1. Heat the oil in a saucepan and fry the chilli and saffron for a minute or so.

2. Add the rice and continue frying and stirring until it is very lightly browned. Add the contents of the can of tomatoes and the water. Stir once and bring to the boil.

3. Arrange the onion and pepper rings on the top, and season. Cover with a lid and cook over a gentle heat for 30 minutes until the rice and vegetables are tender and all the liquid has been absorbed. Serve at once without stirring.

Red Bean Risotto

—◆—

The red beans add colour and flavour to this Italian rice dish but if you do not have a can ready to hand, simply substitute more peas. Use whatever fresh herbs are available.

1 small onion, peeled and chopped
2 garlic cloves, peeled and chopped
1 green pepper, seeded and
* chopped*
50g (2oz) butter, or 3 tablespoons
* olive oil*
350g (12oz) Italian risotto rice
300ml (1/2 pint) dry white wine
1 teaspoon dried mixed herbs
600ml (1 pint) vegetable stock (see
* page xii)*

salt and freshly ground black
* pepper*
50g (2oz) frozen peas
175g (6oz) canned red beans,
* drained*
3 tablespoons freshly chopped
* mixed herbs (basil, tarragon,*
* parsley and chervil)*

1. Sauté the onion, garlic and green pepper in butter or oil until softened.

2. Add the rice and fry gently for 3-4 minutes. Add the wine and bring to the boil. Continue cooking until all the wine is absorbed, stirring from time to time.

3. Add the mixed herbs, vegetable stock and seasoning. Continue cooking until the rice is cooked (about 20-30 minutes), adding more stock if the rice shows signs of drying up completely.

4. Meanwhile cook the frozen peas and add to the cooked risotto with the beans and fresh herbs. Heat through and serve at once.

Millet and Lentil Pilau

—◆—

I like to serve this dish with Roman-Style Spinach (see page 77) and a spicy onion and tomato salad, perhaps with a little soured cream or yoghurt. (Don't buy bird millet, as this has not been cleaned.)

225g (8oz) whole millet
1 tablespoon cooking oil
1 teaspoon cumin seeds
1 small onion, peeled and finely
  chopped

1 garlic clove, peeled and crushed
75g (3oz) split lentils
1 teaspoon ground coriander
600ml (1 pint) vegetable stock (see
  page xii)

1. Dry-fry the millet in a hot non-stick frying pan until well toasted all over. Remove from the pan and keep on one side.

2. Heat the cooking oil in the pan and fry the cumin seeds for 1 minute. Add the onion and garlic and fry until lightly browned.

3. Stir in the lentils, the millet and coriander. Add the stock and bring to the boil. Stir and cover with a lid. Reduce the heat and simmer very gently for 30 minutes. Check to see if more liquid is required, stir and continue cooking for a further 10-15 minutes or until the millet and lentils are fully cooked.

4. Leave to stand for 5 minutes with the lid on, then fluff up and serve.

Mushroom and Walnut Risotto

——◆——

This unusually flavoured risotto is a vegan's dream as it really is much nicer without the usually obligatory Parmesan cheese. However, it is important to use Italian risotto rice.

1 small onion, peeled and sliced	150ml (¹/₄ pint) dry white wine
175g (6oz) button mushrooms, sliced	225g (8oz) Italian risotto rice
	600ml (1 pint) vegetable stock (see page xii)
1 green apple, cored and sliced	
8 half walnuts, cut in half again	salt and freshly ground black pepper
3 tablespoons olive oil	

1. Heat 2 tablespoons of the oil in a large saucepan and fry a quarter of the onion, all the mushrooms, the apple and walnuts for 2-3 minutes. Add the wine and cook for 10 minutes. Drain off the wine and reserve. Remove the vegetables, apple and nuts from the pan and keep warm.

2. Put the remaining oil in the saucepan and fry the remaining onion for 2 minutes. Add the rice and sauté for 2 minutes, stirring constantly. Add the reserved wine and boil until it evaporates, stirring the rice from time to time.

3. Add the vegetable stock and cook without stirring for 25-30 minutes until all the liquid has been taken up.

4. Stir in the reserved onions, mushrooms, apples and walnuts and serve.

Green Risotto

——◆——

This colourful risotto from the plains of Lombardy is delicious served with grated Pecorino cheese.

2 tablespoons olive oil	salt and freshly ground black pepper
2 leeks, trimmed and sliced	
450g (1lb) Swiss chard, shredded	750ml (1¹/₄ pints) very hot vegetable stock (see page xii)
small bunch of parsley, chopped	
225g (8oz) Italian risotto rice	

1. Heat the oil in a pan and gently fry the leeks, Swiss chard and parsley for 5 minutes, stirring occasionally.

2. Add the rice, seasoning and a soup ladleful of stock. Cook over a low to medium heat until the liquid is almost evaporated, stirring from time to time.

3. Add another ladle of stock. Cook until almost evaporated. Repeat, adding more stock and cooking and stirring from time to time, until the rice grains are cooked but still firm. Cook off any remaining liquid. The risotto should be slightly creamy but not wet. Total cooking time from adding the rice will be about 30-35 minutes.

Bulgar Rice
—◆—

The bulgar – also known as *pourgouri* or cracked wheat – gives an interesting texture to this mixed grain dish. Serve it with any of the stir-fry dishes or casserole dishes (see pages 72-83 and 84-102).

175g (6oz) long-grain rice
75g (3oz) bulgar
600ml (1 pint) vegetable stock (see page xii)
salt

25g (1oz) peanuts
25g (1oz) olive oil
2 tablespoons freshly chopped chives

1. Wash the rice and bulgar and drain. Bring the vegetable stock to the boil and add the rice, bulgar and salt. Stir once, cover and simmer for 40-45 minutes until the rice is tender and all the liquid has been taken up. Turn off the heat and leave to stand for 10 minutes before fluffing up with a fork.

2. Meanwhile, fry the nuts in the oil until well browned and sprinkle over the bulgar rice with the chives. Serve at once.

North African Couscous

—◆—

Like pasta, couscous is made from fine semolina, which is mixed with water and made into very small pellets. In North Africa it is steamed over the vegetables in a special pot. Here it is easier to steam on its own in a steamer or in a sieve over a pan of boiling water.

225g (8oz) couscous
350ml (12fl oz) warm water
300ml (½ pint) strong vegetable
  stock (see page xii)
4 carrots, peeled and cut into
  lengths
12 small onions, peeled
4 turnips, peeled and quartered

1 × 415g (14½oz) can of
  chickpeas, drained
125g (4oz) frozen peas
50g (2oz) raisins
1½ teaspoons ground allspice
1 teaspoon ground cumin
salt and freshly ground black
  pepper

1. Soak the couscous in a bowl with the warm water for 10 minutes while you prepare the vegetables.

2. Place the stock in a saucepan and add the carrots, onions and turnips. Simmer for 15 minutes.

3. Add the chickpeas, frozen peas, raisins, allspice, cumin and seasoning and cook for a further 15 minutes.

4. Meanwhile steam the couscous for 20-30 minutes with a lid on top. Make sure that the water does not touch the steamer or the couscous will go lumpy.

5. Stir the cooked couscous with a fork before turning it out on to a large warmed plate. Make a well in the centre and spoon on the vegetable mixture.

Vegetable Tagine

—◆—

A tagine is a spicy stew, traditionally containing dried fruit, from Morocco. It is also the name of the cooking pot in which the stew is cooked. A large saucepan serves the purpose just as well. Serve with couscous.

SERVES 6

225g (8oz) couscous
350ml (12fl oz) warm water
2 tablespoons olive oil
2 onions, peeled and quartered
2 garlic cloves, crushed
3 carrots, peeled and sliced
2 parsnips, peeled and diced
1 teaspoon paprika
$^1/_2$ teaspoon each of ground ginger
   and cinnamon
1 teaspoon each of ground turmeric
   and coriander
125g (4oz) button mushrooms
2 courgettes, trimmed and sliced
125g (4oz) green beans, trimmed
   and cut into 5cm (2in) lengths

750ml (1$^1/_4$ pints) vegetable stock
4 tomatoes, skinned (see page xii),
   deseeded and quartered
425g (15oz) can artichoke hearts,
   drained and halved
425g (15oz) can cannellini beans,
   drained and rinsed
125g (4oz) California prunes,
   stoned (ready-to-eat)
2 tablespoons each of freshly
   chopped parsley and coriander
2 teaspoons clear honey or to taste
salt and freshly ground black
   pepper

1. Soak the couscous in a bowl with the warm water for 10 minutes while you prepare the vegetables.

2. Steam the couscous for 20-30 minutes with a lid on. Make sure the water does not touch the steamer or the couscous will go lumpy.

3. Meanwhile heat oil in a large saucepan, add onions, garlic, carrots and parsnips. Fry gently for 10 minutes then stir in the spices and cook for 1 minute.

4. Add mushrooms, courgettes, green beans and stock. Bring to the boil then cook for 10 minutes. Add tomatoes, artichoke hearts, cannellini beans, prunes and herbs. Cook for a further 10 minutes or until vegetables are tender. Add honey and seasonings to taste.

5. Stir the cooked couscous with a fork before turning it out onto four individual warm plates. Make a well in the centre and spoon on the vegetables.

Dry-Fried Okra with Bulgar

—◆—

Unlike some dishes using okra the result here is quite dry. No liquid is added to the dish and any stickiness from the sliced okra seems to be taken up by the bulgar. Add 125g (4oz) cooked broad beans at the last minute for a more substantial dish. If you like to have a sauce with your food, serve with one of the stir-fry or casserole dishes (see pages 72-83 and 84-102).

50g (2oz) bulgar
1 tablespoon cooking oil
3 spring onions, very finely
  chopped
1 red pepper, seeded and very finely
  chopped

300g (10oz) okra, trimmed and
  thinly sliced
salt and freshly ground black
  pepper

1. Cover the bulgar with cold water and leave to stand for 30 minutes. Drain and dry very well on kitchen paper.

2. Heat the oil in the wok or frying pan and fry the spring onion and pepper for 1 minute. Add the okra and continue to stir-fry for another 2 minutes.

3. Add the dried bulgar and seasoning. Toss over a very high heat until the bulgar begins to brown slightly. Serve at once.

Baked Barley with Mushrooms

—◆—

This recipe uses pot barley or whole-grain barley. It is not designed for pearl barley which does not really have very much in the way of nutrients anyway.

1 large onion, peeled and finely
  chopped
2 tablespoons cooking oil
1 carrot, peeled and grated
225g (8oz) button mushrooms,
  sliced
175g (6oz) pot barley, washed and
  drained

250ml (8fl oz) vegetable stock (see
  page xii)
1/2 teaspoon dried marjoram or
  oregano
salt and freshly ground black
  pepper

1. Preheat the oven to 180°C/350°F/Gas 4.

2. Heat the oil in a casserole dish and fry the onion for 2-3 minutes. Add the carrot and mushrooms and continue cooking for another 3-4 minutes until the vegetables begin to soften.

3. Stir in the barley then add all the remaining ingredients and bake for 1 hour until the barley is cooked through.

STIR-FRY DISHES

In China, stir-frying is a very quick process which does not use much fat. The temperatures used are very high and difficult to reproduce at home. The answer is to use a non-stick wok with no more than a couple of tablespoons of oil. It is actually possible to stir-fry with no oil at all, but in 3-4 tablespoons of stock. If you try this, keep the heat turned up high to boil off the liquid.

Most of the dishes in this section are indeed very quick to prepare. They can be served with rice or Chinese noodles, but they also make a very good topping for pasta or a filling for jacket potatoes.

I like to serve two or three at once, which looks attractive and adds interest to the plate. As a result, the quantities given here are based on the idea that at least two will be served at once. If you only have time to make one dish, the quantities will serve two hungry people.

Gujerati Cabbage

This is a very quick spicy vegetable dish which is served as an everyday item in the Indian State of Gujerat. Any kind of cabbage can be pressed into service.

2 tablespoons pure corn oil
1 teaspoon whole cumin seeds
1 teaspoon whole black or yellow
    mustard seeds
1 onion, peeled and sliced
175g (6oz) green or white cabbage,
    very finely chopped
75g (3oz) red cabbage, very finely
    chopped

125g (4oz) carrots, peeled and
    coarsely grated
1/2 small fresh green chilli, seeded
    and cut into very thin strips
1/2 teaspoon salt
a pinch of sugar
2 heaped tablespoons freshly
    chopped coriander
1 tablespoon lemon juice

1. Heat the oil in a frying pan and fry the whole spices until they begin to pop.

2. Quickly add the onion and then the cabbage, carrots and green chilli, and turn the heat down to medium. Stir-fry the vegetables for 5 minutes.

3. Add all the remaining ingredients except the lemon juice and cook for a further 10 minutes covered with a lid. Stir from time to time.

4. Just before serving pour on the lemon juice and toss the vegetables well.

Courgettes with Pine Kernels and Orange
—◆—

The courgettes take up the flavour of the orange very well. Serve with Broad Beans in *Tahina* Sauce or Leeks with Cashew Nuts (see page 75).

6-8 spring onions, trimmed and chopped
2 tablespoons olive oil
450g (1lb) courgettes, trimmed and sliced
3 tablespoons pine kernels, toasted (see page xiii)

juice and finely grated rind of 1 large orange
1 tablespoon freshly chopped dill
salt and freshly ground black pepper

1. Fry the onions in oil for 1 minute then add the courgettes, and stir-fry for 2 minutes.

2. Add all the remaining ingredients, and toss over a high heat until most of the juice has evaporated. Serve at once.

Tofu with Cashew Nuts
——◆——

It is worth remembering that *tofu* is a good substitute for dairy food. It behaves in much the same way, but contains no saturated fat. Any kind of vegetables in season can be used in this recipe. Good alternative combinations include mangetout with baby sweetcorn and carrots; green peppers with bamboo shoots; and fennel or broccoli with red chilli peppers and celeriac.

2 tablespoons cooking oil
1 garlic clove, peeled and finely chopped
3 teaspoons freshly grated root ginger
225g (8oz) tofu, cut into strips
1/2 bunch spring onions, trimmed and cut into lengths
2 carrots, peeled and cut into thin sticks

125g (4oz) French beans, topped and tailed
1 × 225g (8oz) can of water chestnuts, drained and sliced
3 tablespoons vegetable stock (see page xii)
1 tablespoon soy sauce
25g (1oz) cashew nuts, toasted
1 tablespoon pine kernels, toasted (see page xiii)

1. Heat 1 tablespoon of the cooking oil in a wok or deep frying pan, and gently fry the garlic and half the ginger.

2. Add the *tofu* and carefully stir-fry for about a minute, then remove from the pan.

3. Add the remaining oil and ginger to the pan with all the vegetables and the water chestnuts. Stir-fry for 2-3 minutes.

4. Pour in the stock and soy sauce and toss over a high heat for 1 minute. Reduce the heat and cover with a lid and cook for a further 1-2 minutes.

5. Add the cashew nuts, pine kernels and *tofu*, and toss over a low heat. Serve at once.

Broad Beans in Tahina Sauce

—◆—

Tahina is a paste of crushed sesame seeds in their own oil. It usually needs to be diluted with lemon juice or water. The longer you cook this sauce the thicker it will become. One minute in the wok or pan should be sufficient to heat it through without thickening too much.

300g (10oz) fresh or frozen broad
  beans
6-8 spring onions, trimmed and
  chopped
1 tablespoon cooking oil

3 tablespoons tahina *(sesame seed*
  paste)
150ml (¹/4 pint) water
salt and freshly ground black
  pepper

1. Cook the beans in salted boiling water until just tender.

2. Stir-fry the spring onions in the oil for 1 minute. Add the beans and toss well together.

3. Gradually mix the *tahina* with the water to form a smooth cream. Season, then pour over the beans and heat through.

Leeks with Cashew Nuts

—◆—

The flavour of leeks seems to merge well with that of the celery in this very quickly made dish. Serve with pasta spirals and one other sauce or topping.

1 large head of celery, trimmed and
  sliced
3-4 leeks, trimmed and sliced
¹/4 garlic clove, peeled and chopped
2 tablespoons olive oil
3 tablespoons cashew nuts, toasted

2 tablespoons freshly chopped
  parsley
1 tablespoon freshly chopped basil
salt and freshly ground black
  pepper

1. Stir-fry the celery, leek and garlic in the oil for 2-3 minutes.

2. Add all the remaining ingredients. Toss well to heat through and serve at once.

Spiced Yams

—◆—

This is a variation on a Spanish recipe for spiced potatoes. In fact it is very good made with both regular and sweet potatoes as well as with yams.

700g (1¹/₂lb) yams, peeled and
   cubed
a little lemon juice
1 onion, peeled and finely chopped
1 tablespoon cooking oil

3 red chilli peppers, seeded and
   chopped
¹/₂ teaspoon allspice
a pinch of grated nutmeg
salt and freshly ground black
   pepper

1. Cook the yams with the lemon juice in salted boiling water for about 15 minutes until tender. Drain well.

2. Meanwhile fry the onion in the cooking oil until lightly browned.

3. Add all the remaining ingredients and the yams. Fry for 3-4 minutes, turning from time to time.

Stir-Fried Broccoli with *Tofu*

—◆—

This oriental recipe uses purple sprouting broccoli rather than the more compact calabrese. My father grows it in his garden and there is always more than he knows what to do with!

50g (2oz) flaked almonds
1 tablespoon cooking oil
1 onion, peeled and thinly sliced
450g (1lb) purple sprouting
   broccoli, washed and cut into
   lengths

125g (4oz) tofu, *diced*
1 tablespoon soy sauce
a pinch of five-spice powder

1. Toast the flaked almonds in a dry frying pan to brown them. Remove from the pan and keep on one side.

2. Add the cooking oil to the pan and stir-fry the onion for 1 minute. Add the broccoli and continue stir-frying for a further 2 minutes.

3. Add the *tofu*, soy sauce and five-spice powder and cook for a further minute. Serve at once. The broccoli should still be quite crunchy.

Roman-Style Spinach
——◆——

I love this dish simply served with rice or pasta, but it can also be used to accompany a variety of other dishes. It is really important to squeeze out as much liquid as possible from the cooked spinach before stir-frying it, otherwise it will be rather watery.

700g (1¹/₂lb) spinach, after
*   trimming off thick stalks*
1 garlic clove, peeled and roughly
*   sliced*
3 tablespoons olive oil

2 tablespoons pine kernels
2 tablespoons raisins, soaked in
*   warm water for 15 minutes, and*
*   drained*
salt and freshly ground black
*   pepper*

1. Wash the spinach well, shake to remove most of the water, then cook in a large pan with no added water. Squeeze dry.

2. Fry the garlic and pine kernels in the oil until browned. Remove the pine kernels and keep on one side.

3. Toss the spinach and drained raisins in the oil until well coated and then add the pine kernels. Toss over heat for 3-4 minutes and serve.

Beetroot with Dill

—◆—

Beetroot takes well to other strong flavours and I vary this recipe, depending on my mood, by sometimes adding ½ teaspoon grated orange rind or garlic or whole cumin seeds.

1 tablespoon cooking oil
½ teaspoon grated orange rind or
   garlic or whole cumin seeds
   (optional)
2 large cooked beetroot, peeled and
   diced

4 tablespoons plain yoghurt
6-8 sprigs of fresh dill
salt and freshly ground black
   pepper

1. Heat the oil in a wok or pan and fry your chosen flavouring, if any.

2. Add the beetroot and toss in the oil for 2-3 minutes.

3. Add all the remaining ingredients and toss over a fairly high heat until the sauce thickens.

Stir-Fried Mixed Beans

—◆—

This dish is both colourful and tasty. Of course, other kinds of beans can be substituted, depending on the contents of your store cupboard and the fresh beans on sale in the shops.

1 small onion, peeled and finely
   chopped
1 garlic clove, peeled and crushed
   (optional)
2 tablespoons groundnut oil
225g (8oz) green beans, trimmed
   and cut into lengths
125g (4oz) podded broad beans
125g (4oz) canned red kidney
   beans, drained

4 tablespoons vegetable stock (see
   page xii)
½ teaspoon grated lemon rind
2 tablespoons freshly chopped
   parsley
salt and freshly ground black
   pepper

1. Fry the onion and garlic in the oil for 2 minutes, then add the green beans and broad beans. Stir-fry for 2-3 minutes.

2. Add all the remaining ingredients. Bring to the boil and cook over a high heat for a further 1-2 minutes, stirring all the time.

Green Beans with Halloumi Cheese
— ◆ —

Most cheeses cannot be used in a stir-fry because they melt. Halloumi, on the other hand, tends to stiffen with heat. However, take care not to cook for too long, as it can get quite tough.

3 tablespoons cooking oil
a few drops of oriental sesame oil
350g (12oz) green beans, trimmed
   and sliced
2 leeks, trimmed and sliced

125g (4oz) Halloumi cheese, cut
   into thin strips
freshly ground black pepper
1 tablespoon sesame seeds, toasted
   (see page xiii)

1. Heat 2 tablespoons of the cooking oil with the sesame oil in a wok or deep frying pan, and stir-fry the beans for 2 minutes. Add the leeks and continue stir-frying for another 1-2 minutes. Transfer the vegetables to a warmed dish.

2. Heat the remaining cooking oil and stir-fry the cheese for about a minute.

3. Return the vegetables to the pan and toss well together. Serve sprinkled with black pepper and toasted sesame seeds.

Greek Cheese Squares with Olives

—◆—

I often serve this colourful chunky mixture on large pieces of toasted Greek or Italian bread instead of on a bed of rice or pasta.

2 tablespoons cooking oil
6 spring onions, trimmed and finely chopped
1 garlic clove, peeled and crushed
175g (6oz) Halloumi cheese, cut into squares
12-16 black olives, pitted

a pinch of dried thyme or oregano
4 tomatoes, cut into wedges or coarsely chopped
4 tablespoons chopped fresh basil
salt and freshly ground black pepper

1. Heat the oil in a wok or deep frying pan and stir-fry the onion and garlic for 1 minute.

2. Add all the remaining ingredients and toss over a medium heat for about another minute. Serve as soon as the tomatoes have warmed through.

Mixed Root Vegetable Sticks in Soy Sauce

—◆—

The secret of this simple dish is to combine the vegetables with complementary flavours. The ginger, sherry and soy go well with root vegetables. As well as those given below I like to use beetroot and swede or parsnips and carrots.

3 tablespoons cooking oil
1 small onion, peeled and finely sliced
1 garlic clove, peeled
1 teaspoon freshly grated root ginger
1 large potato, peeled and cut into thin sticks
1/2 medium celeriac, peeled and cut into thin sticks

2 carrots, peeled and cut into thin sticks
4 tablespoons vegetable stock (see page xii)
1 tablespoon soy sauce
1 tablespoon sherry
freshly ground black pepper

1. Heat the oil in a wok or deep frying pan and stir-fry the onion, garlic and ginger for 2 minutes.

2. Add the potato and stir-fry for another 2 minutes.

3. Add the other vegetables and continue stir-frying for 2-3 minutes.

4. Add all the remaining ingredients and bring to the boil. Cover with a lid and cook for a further 2-3 minutes, stirring from time to time until the potato is cooked through and most of the liquid has evaporated.

Fried Noodles

——◆——

Fried noodles make a change from rice and can be served with any of the stir-fried dishes in this chapter. They can also make a good dish in their own right if you add one or two of the suggested flavourings given below. Prepare any chosen flavouring in advance.

225g (8oz) Chinese dried egg
   noodles
3-4 tablespoons cooking oil

1 teaspoon soy sauce
freshly ground black pepper

1. Cook the noodles as directed on the pack. Drain very well before frying.

2. Heat the oil in a wok or deep frying pan and add the noodles. Stir-fry for 1 minute. Add the soy sauce and pepper and toss well. If you are using some of the flavourings prepare in advance and add at this stage.

Suggested flavourings

1 red pepper, seeded, cut into strips and stir-fried with 1 tablespoon toasted almonds.

or

1/2 bunch watercress with the segments of 1 orange, chopped, and 1 teaspoon sesame seeds.

or

225g (8oz) mangetout stir-fried with 1 teaspoon chopped fresh root ginger.

Noodles with Indonesian Sauce

—◆—

This tasty, peanut-flavoured noodle dish is quick to prepare and fun to eat. Serve with spicy chutney and a green salad.

225g (8oz) Chinese dried egg
 noodles
2 tablespoons cooking oil
1cm (1/2in) piece of fresh root
 ginger, peeled and cut into thin
 strips
2 onions, peeled and sliced
1 large red or green pepper, seeded
 and sliced
350g (12oz) Chinese cabbage
 leaves, sliced
125g (4oz) beansprouts

3 tablespoons salted peanuts
1 tablespoon soy sauce

Sauce
3 tablespoons peanut butter
175ml (6fl oz) hot water
1 teaspoon black treacle or
 molasses
2 tablespoons soy sauce
1/2 garlic clove, peeled and crushed
3 tablespoons lemon juice

1. To make the sauce, mix the peanut butter with the hot water. Stir in all the remaining ingredients and bring to the boil. Stir and keep warm.

2. Plunge the noodles into boiling water and turn off the heat. Leave to stand for 5 minutes.

3. Heat the cooking oil in a wok or a deep frying pan and quickly stir-fry the root ginger and onion. Add the peppers and continue to stir-fry for 2-3 minutes. Add the Chinese cabbage, beansprouts and peanuts. Toss over the heat for a further 2-3 minutes. The vegetables should soften but remain crisp in the centre.

4. Drain the noodles well and toss with the vegetables. Sprinkle on the soy sauce and serve with the peanut sauce.

opposite: Vegetable Tagine (page 69)

Fresh Ratatouille

——◆——

Ratatouille is probably one of the most popular Mediterranean vegetable dishes. This fresh tasting version includes broad beans. Serve with rice or bulgar wheat.

1 tablespoon olive oil
225g (8oz) onions, peeled and
*   chopped*
1 clove garlic, peeled and crushed
1 red pepper, seeded and chopped
1 yellow pepper, seeded and
*   chopped*
1 aubergine, chopped

100g (4oz) courgettes, trimmed
*   and sliced*
2 tablespoons tomato purée
150ml (¹/₄ pint) dry white wine
salt and freshly ground black
*   pepper*
100g (4oz) broad beans

1. Fry all the vegetables, except the broad beans, in the olive oil.

2. After 3-4 minutes add the tomato purée, wine and salt and pepper. Cook for about 15 minutes then add the broad beans and cook for a further 10 minutes.

opposite, clockwise from the top: Pasta Ribbons with Sautéed Spring Vegetables (page 45), Chinese Money Bags (page 163) and Fresh Ratatouille (above) on a bed of bulgar wheat

BAKES AND CASSEROLES

This section contains a collection of dishes which might be baked in the oven or stewed on the hob. Many of them are quite quick to prepare, you can then leave them to cook. Dishes like Potato Stew, Russian Cabbage Pie, Tortino di Zucchini, Malaysian Vegetable Fruit Curry, Vegetarian Chilli, African Curried Vegetables and Fennel Bean Pot only need the addition of rice, potatoes, bulgar or bread to complete the meal.

Other dishes can be baked together or served with dishes from other sections. Ideas are given in the menu planning section on page xiii-xiv.

Potato Stew

This is a favourite winter dish from my childhood. My mother would serve steaming bowls of it topped with a mixture of freshly grated carrot and cheese.

3 onions, peeled and sliced
2 tablespoons cooking oil
4-5 tablespoons fine or medium
   oatmeal
750ml (1¹/₄ pints) vegetable stock
   (see page xii)

1 heaped tablespoon yeast extract
4-6 large potatoes, peeled and cut
   into chunks
salt and freshly ground black
   pepper

1. Fry the onions in cooking oil until golden.

2. Add the oatmeal and continue cooking for a few minutes, then add the stock and yeast extract. Bring to the boil.

3. Add the chopped potatoes and seasoning, and simmer for 30 minutes, stirring from time to time until the potatoes are cooked. Add a little more stock if the stew gets too thick.

Spiced Potatoes

—◆—

These delicately spiced potatoes go with all kinds of food, not just Indian food. Yoghurt generally requires the addition of flour to prevent it separating in cooking. This isn't necessary here because most of the liquid evaporates during cooking.

1 tablespoon cooking oil	freshly ground black pepper
1 teaspoon whole cumin seeds	700g (1¹/₂lb) potatoes, peeled and
¹/₂ teaspoon curry powder	cubed
¹/₄ teaspoon ground bay leaf	150g (5oz) plain yoghurt
¹/₄ teaspoon celery salt	

1. Heat the cooking oil in a good-sized pan and fry the cumin seeds for about a minute. Add the rest of the herbs and spices and fry for a little longer.

2. Add the potatoes and stir to make sure that they are well coated with the spices.

3. Pour on the yoghurt, stir, and bring to the boil. Cover and simmer for 20-30 minutes, stirring occasionally, until the potatoes are tender and most of the liquid has been absorbed.

Baked Sweet Potatoes

—◆—

This American speciality from the Deep South has quite a sweet flavour which goes well with Russian Cabbage Pie or Artichokes Jerusalem (see pages 87 and 91).

4 small sweet potatoes, washed and
    dried
50g (2oz) butter
25g (1oz) brown sugar
salt

1 tablespoon sherry
$1/2 \times 225g$ (8oz) can of pineapple
    slices, drained
$1/4$ teaspoon grated nutmeg
25g (1oz) raisins

1. Preheat the oven to 190°C/375°F/Gas 5.

2. Bake the sweet potatoes for about an hour until tender. Cut off the tops, scoop out the flesh and mash with a fork.

3. Place the butter, sugar, a little salt and the sherry in a saucepan and heat gently, stirring all the time. When the sugar has dissolved and the butter melted, add the pineapple, nutmeg and raisins.

4. Mix with the mashed potato. Pile the mixture back into the potato skins, return to the oven and bake for a further 10 minutes.

Braised Cabbage with Grapefruit

—◆—

This unusual combination of flavours works very well. The recipe comes from an old cookery book belonging to my grandmother.

$1/2$ large green Savoy cabbage,
    shredded
2 Granny Smith apples, peeled,
    cored and chopped

juice of 1 grapefruit
300g (10oz) plain yoghurt
salt and freshly ground black
    pepper

1. Preheat the oven to 200°C/400°F/Gas 6.

2. Mix the cabbage and apples together and place in a casserole dish. Pour the grapefruit juice over the top, cover and bake for 45 minutes.

3. Stir in the yoghurt and seasoning, cover again and continue cooking for a further 15 minutes.

Russian Cabbage Pie

—◆—

This pie, flavoured with caraway and cardamom, can be topped with shortcrust pastry instead of mashed potatoes.

1/2 teaspoon caraway seeds
seeds from 4 cardamom pods
300ml (1/2 pint) soured cream
50g (2oz) butter
1kg (2lb) white cabbage, finely
  shredded
salt and freshly ground black
  pepper

225g (8oz) cooked beetroot, diced
4 hard-boiled eggs, shelled and
  sliced
700g (11/2lb) potatoes, peeled and
  cooked
milk

1. Crush the caraway and cardamom seeds together in a mortar. Mix with the soured cream and keep on one side.

2. Melt 25g (1oz) of the butter in a large pan and add the cabbage. Fry gently for 3-4 minutes until the cabbage softens. Pour on the spiced soured cream and season. Cover with a lid and cook over a low heat for 40 minutes, stirring occasionally.

3. Meanwhile, preheat the oven to 200°C/400°F/Gas 6.

4. Mix the beetroot into the cabbage and transfer the mixture to a casserole or pie dish. Arrange a layer of hard-boiled egg slices over the top and add a little more seasoning. Mash the potatoes with the remaining butter and a little milk, and spread over the dish, forking the top into an attractive pattern. Bake for 15-20 minutes.

Cabbage Lorraine

—◆—

The French province of Lorraine borders on Germany, and many of the culinary traditions are similar. Here the caraway seeds, popular in Germany, are used with a French accent. The recipe can also be made using Chinese leaves

1 small or ¹/₂ large cabbage, cut
   into wedges
1 small onion, peeled and sliced
25g (1oz) butter
2 tomatoes, skinned (see page xiii)
   and chopped
a large pinch of caraway seeds

15g (¹/₂oz) flour
300ml (¹/₂ pint) vegetable stock (see
   page xii) or water
salt and freshly ground black
   pepper
3 tablespoons soured cream
1 tablespoon chopped parsley

1. Preheat the oven to 180°C/350°F/Gas 4.

2. Blanch the wedges of cabbage in lightly salted boiling water for 7-8 minutes. Place in a casserole.

3. Fry the onion in the butter until very lightly browned. Add the tomatoes and continue frying for a minute or so. Stir in the caraway seeds, flour and then the stock. Continue cooking and stirring until the mixture thickens.

4. Add the seasoning, then pour the sauce over the cabbage, and bake for 45 minutes, basting occasionally.

5. Pour the soured cream over the top and bake for a further 15 minutes. Serve, sprinkled with parsley.

Cabbage and Onion Casserole

—◆—

Any kind of cabbage can be used for this substantial vegetable casserole. Turn it into a main course by adding 75g (3oz) uncooked rice and 3 tablespoons of vegetable stock to the mix, and serve with plenty of grated cheese sprinkled over each portion.

450g (1lb) cabbage, shredded
3 large onions, peeled and sliced
1 leek, washed and sliced (optional)
50g (2oz) butter

2 tablespoons freshly chopped mint
  or dill, or 1/4 teaspoon cumin or
  caraway seeds
salt and freshly ground black
  pepper

1. Preheat the oven to 190°C/375°F/Gas 5.

2. Layer the vegetables in a casserole dish adding a few knobs of butter and a sprinkling of herbs or spices and seasoning to each layer. Finish with a layer of cabbage.

3. Cover with a lid and bake for about an hour until the vegetables are tender.

Braised Red Cabbage

——◆——

The oranges and raisins in this recipe complement the red cabbage well, and give an unusual flavour to the finished dish.

1 onion, peeled and sliced
1 tablespoon cooking oil
450g (1lb) red cabbage, finely
  shredded
25g (1oz) raisins

juice and finely grated rind of 1
  orange
2 tablespoons redcurrant jelly
2 tablespoons cider vinegar

1. Fry the onion in cooking oil for about 4-5 minutes until softened and lightly browned.

2. Add the cabbage and continue cooking and stirring occasionally for a further 10 minutes.

3. Mix the remaining ingredients and add to the pan. Stir well and bring to the boil. Cover and simmer for 45-50 minutes until the cabbage is tender and most of the liquid has been taken up.

Stewed Beetroot with Onions
—◆—

Beetroot is one of my favourite vegetables and I particularly like it hot. This recipe is quite spicy, but if you prefer something a little milder, use the juice and rind of 1 orange in place of the cumin, garlic and tomato purée. Use cooked beetroot for a speedier result; this cuts the cooking time to 15-20 minutes.

2 tablespoons cooking oil
1 teaspoon whole cumin seeds
1 garlic clove, peeled and crushed
2 onions, peeled and sliced
salt and freshly ground black
*   pepper*

4 small beetroot (450g/1lb in
*   total), peeled and cut into*
*   wedges*
2 tablespoons tomato purée
juice of 1 lemon
50ml (2fl oz) water

1. Heat the cooking oil in a pan and fry the cumin seeds and garlic for 1 minute. Add the onion and fry for a further 2-3 minutes.

2. Add all the remaining ingredients, bring to the boil and simmer, covered, for 50 minutes, or until the beetroot is tender. Stir from time to time.

Creamy Artichoke Casserole
—◆—

Jerusalem artichokes are a nuisance to prepare because they are so knobbly. However, a new variety has been developed with a smoother shape. This dish makes a very good accompaniment to Fennel Bean Pot or Braised Leeks with Courgettes (see pages 102 and 95).

700g (1¹/₂lb) Jerusalem artichokes,
*   well scrubbed*
2 onions, peeled
3 tablespoons low-fat soft cheese

salt and freshly ground black
*   pepper*
4 tablespoons wholemeal
*   breadcrumbs*

1. Steam the artichokes and the whole onions in a steamer for about 35-40 minutes until the artichokes are soft, or boil in a little water for about 20-25 minutes. Drain both, and peel the artichokes.

2. Preheat the oven to 190°C/375°F/Gas 5.

3. Mash the onions and peeled artichokes together. Stir in the cream cheese, and season.

4. Spoon into a casserole or pie dish, sprinkle with breadcrumbs, and bake for 30 minutes.

Artichokes Jerusalem
—◆—

This recipe uses Jerusalem artichokes in a manner which might well be found in the city of their name.

1 large onion, peeled and chopped
2 tablespoons olive oil
700g (1¹/₂lb) large Jerusalem
* artichokes*
4 tomatoes, skinned (see page xiii)
* and chopped*
1 tablespoon tomato purée

¹/₂ teaspoon dried dill
salt and freshly ground black
* pepper*
juice of 1 lemon
2 tablespoons chopped parsley
150ml (¹/₄ pint) water

1. Fry the onion in hot olive oil until well browned.

2. Meanwhile wash and peel the artichokes and wash again. Cut into quarters and add to the onion. Toss well so that they are coated in oil.

3. Add all the remaining ingredients, stir and bring to the boil. Cover and simmer, stirring from time to time, for 30-35 minutes until the artichokes are just tender and the sauce is thick.

Celery with Provence Herbs

———◆———

I discovered this dish in a restaurant just under the walls of the Roman amphitheatre in Orange. It uses classic Provence herbs which include fennel seeds – the secret here. It's equally good served hot or cold. For the cold version simply add a tablespoon of lemon juice or cider vinegar.

1 head of celery, trimmed and sliced
1 onion, peeled and finely sliced
1 tablespoon cooking oil
1 tomato, skinned (see page xiii) seeded and chopped (optional)
1 tablespoon tomato purée
¹/₄ teaspoon fennel seeds

2 sprigs fresh rosemary, or ¹/₄ teaspoon dried rosemary
2 sprigs fresh thyme, or ¹/₄ teaspoon dried thyme
salt and freshly ground black pepper
1 tablespoon lemon juice or cider vinegar (if serving cold)

1. Steam the celery in a steamer, or boil in a very little salted boiling water until tender. This will take about 20-30 minutes depending on the size and age of the celery.

2. Meanwhile gently fry the onion in the cooking oil until it turns transparent. Add the tomato and tomato purée and all the herbs and seasoning. Continue cooking gently for about 8-10 minutes, adding a little water if the mixture shows signs of getting too dry.

3. When the celery is cooked, drain well and mix with the dressing. Serve hot or leave to cool and add a tablespoon of lemon juice or cider vinegar.

Celeriac and Tomato Casserole
—◆—

Celeriac tends to be a rather under-rated vegetable but it has a lovely flavour which is reminiscent of celery and parsnips. Take care when preparing as it discolours quite quickly. Rub cut surfaces with lemon or drop into water with a little lemon juice or vinegar added to it.

1 onion, peeled and sliced
1 tablespoon cooking oil
1 medium celeriac, peeled and
   diced
1 × 400g (14oz) can of tomatoes

$^1/_4$ teaspoon grated lemon rind
juice of $^1/_2$ lemon
a pinch of mixed herbs
salt and freshly ground black
   pepper

1. Gently fry the onion in cooking oil for about 3-4 minutes until it turns transparent.

2. Add the celeriac and continue to fry gently for a further 2-3 minutes.

3. Add all the remaining ingredients and bring to the boil. Simmer for 40 minutes until the celeriac is tender and the sauce is fairly thick.

Lettuce with Spring Onions and Peas
—◆—

This is a good dish to make with the very first fresh peas. The other ingredients help to make a few peas go quite a lot further.

1 medium head of crisp lettuce
1 bunch of spring onions, trimmed
175g (6oz) peas
a knob of butter

$^1/_2$-1 teaspoon sugar
3 tablespoons water
2 sprigs of parsley

1. Cut the lettuce into quarters, wash and drain very well.

2. Place all the ingredients in a saucepan and bring to the boil. Cover and reduce the heat. Cook very gently for about 20 minutes until all the vegetables are tender.

3. Transfer to a warmed serving dish. Remove the parsley and serve.

Persian-Style Okra

—◆—

Okra is one of the basic vegetables of Iraq (formerly Persia) and is used in all kinds of dishes from soups to stews. This is good served with any spicy dishes

450g (1lb) okra
1 large onion, peeled and sliced
1 garlic clove, peeled and chopped
1 tablespoon olive oil
4 tomatoes, skinned (see page xiii) and chopped

$^1/_2$ teaspoon ground coriander
$^1/_4$ teaspoon turmeric
salt and freshly ground black pepper
juice of $^1/_2$ lemon

1. Cut the stems off the okra, taking care not to cut into the main body of the vegetable.

2. Fry the onion and garlic in the olive oil until very lightly browned. Add the okra and gently fry with the onions for a minute or two.

3. Add all the remaining ingredients. Bring to the boil, cover and simmer for about 20-30 minutes until the okra is tender. Take care not to overcook, or the okra will go mushy and slimy.

Marrow Hongroise

—◆—

One of my favourite Hungarian restaurants in London serves marrow this way and, after some persuasion, the chef finally consented to part with the recipe.

1 medium vegetable marrow
1 small onion, sliced and fried in a little butter
2 tablespoons freshly chopped dill, or 1 tablespoon dried dill

1 large sweet and sour gherkin, sliced
1 tablespoon vegetable stock (see page xii) or water
6 tablespoons double cream

1. Preheat the oven to 190°C/375°F/Gas 5.

2. Peel the marrow and then cut in half and remove the seeds. Cut into small cubes.

94

3. Mix the marrow with the fried onion, dill and gherkin and place in a casserole dish with the water or stock. Cover and bake for 45 minutes.

4. Drain off the cooking liquor and mix it with the cream. Pour into a saucepan and bring to the boil. Continue boiling for 3-4 minutes, then when the mixture thickens, pour over the marrow and serve.

Braised Leeks with Courgettes
—◆—

Baked leeks retain their flavour very much more than if they are steamed or boiled. Serve with Potato and Mushroom Celeste or Savoury Baked Rice (see pages 106 and 57).

1 tablespoon olive oil
6 large leeks, washed and trimmed
1 onion, peeled and sliced
1 tablespoon tomato purée
4 tablespoons water

salt and freshly ground black pepper
225g (8oz) courgettes, trimmed and sliced

1. Preheat the oven to 190°C/375°F/Gas 5.

2. Heat the oil in a frying pan until very hot. Cut the leeks into 2.5cm (1 in) lengths and toss into the pan. Quickly brown and transfer to a small casserole. Next fry the onion and add to the leeks.

3. Mix together the tomato purée and water and pour over the vegetables. Season and cover. Bake for 30 minutes.

4. Add the courgettes, and continue cooking for a further 15 minutes.

Vegetarian Chilli

——◆——

This delicious alternative to the original TexMex dish gains in complementary protein if served with a rice dish. It goes well with a mixture of vegetarian Indian dishes, such as Aloo Gobi (see page 101), curried okra or aubergines, rice and Raita (see page 169).

1 onion, peeled and finely chopped
1 garlic clove, peeled and finely chopped
3 tablespoons polyunsaturated cooking oil
225g (8oz) mushrooms, finely chopped
1 medium aubergine, finely diced

2 tablespoons tomato purée
150ml ($^1/_4$ pint) red or white wine
3-4 tablespoons water or stock
1-2 teaspoons chilli powder to taste
$^1/_2$ teaspoon ground cumin
a pinch of mixed herbs
1 × 300g (10oz) can of red kidney beans, drained

1. Fry the onion and garlic in hot oil until lightly browned or softened. Add the mushrooms and continue cooking for 3-4 minutes, stirring all the time.

2. Add all the remaining ingredients except the beans and bring to the boil. Reduce the heat and simmer for 30 minutes.

3. Stir in the beans and cook for a further 10 minutes.

Malaysian Vegetable Fruit Curry

——◆——

Tamarind and lemongrass contribute a lovely lemony flavour in this mild curry from South-East Asia. At a pinch you could use one or the other or, if you cannot find them at all, substitute lemon juice. The flavour will not be quite the same but it will still be very good.

1 tablespoon freshly grated root
   ginger
2 garlic cloves, peeled and crushed
2 pieces lemongrass
1 onion, peeled and sliced
1 tablespoon cooking oil
1 tablespoon tamarind paste, seeds
   removed
1 tablespoon curry powder

300-450ml (^{1}/$_2$-^{3}/$_4$ pint) vegetable
   stock (see page xii)
700g (1^1/$_2$lb) mixed vegetables
   (carrots, potatoes, green beans,
   mouli radish, peas and
   cauliflower)
2 tablespoons raisins
1 × 200g (7oz) can of pineapple
   chunks, drained

1. Fry the ginger, garlic, lemongrass and onion in cooking oil for 2-3 minutes. Stir in the tamarind paste, curry powder and vegetable stock, and bring to the boil.

2. Add all the vegetables except the cauliflower, and simmer for 35-45 minutes.

3. Add the cauliflower, raisins and pineapple chunks and cook for a further 10 minutes.

Tarka Dhal

—◆—

This punchy version of Indian lentil *dhal* goes with any curry. It is also very good if it is cooked a little longer and served in *taco* shells with shredded lettuce and grated cheese.

125g (4oz) lentils
600ml (1 pint) water
1 teaspoon turmeric
salt
1 small onion, peeled and sliced

2 garlic cloves, peeled and crushed
2.5cm (1in) piece of fresh root
   ginger, peeled and grated
1 tablespoon cooking oil

1. Place the lentils in a pan with the water, bring to the boil, and simmer for 45 minutes.

2. Add the turmeric and some salt and continue cooking until the lentils are really soft (about another 30 minutes).

3. Fry the onion, garlic and ginger in the cooking oil until well browned. Add to the *dhal* just before serving.

Tortino di Zucchini

—◆—

I owe a debt of thanks to Anna del Conte for the idea for this Italian-based dish of courgettes and tomatoes. Chopped nuts can be used instead of the cheese.

700g (1¹/₂lb) courgettes, trimmed
salt
2 small onions, peeled and sliced
3 garlic cloves, peeled and chopped
2 tablespoons olive oil
1 × 425g (15 oz) can of tomatoes,
    coarsely chopped or puréed
2 tablespoons freshly chopped
    parsley

leaves from 1 large sprig of fresh
    basil
freshly ground black pepper
40g (1¹/₂oz) rye bread, made into
    breadcrumbs
50g (2oz) Pecorino or hard goat's
    cheese, grated

1. Slice the courgettes fairly thickly and place in a colander over a plate. Sprinkle generously with salt and leave to stand.

2. Gently fry the onion and garlic in the olive oil to soften and lightly brown. Add the tomatoes, herbs and pepper and bring to the boil. Simmer for 15-20 minutes until fairly thick.

3. Preheat the oven to 200°C/400°F/Gas 6.

4. Wash the courgettes under plenty of running water. Drain and pat dry with kitchen towels. Add to the tomato sauce and cook for about 10 minutes until *al dente*. Transfer to an ovenproof dish.

5. Mix the crumbs and cheese and sprinkle over the dish. Place in the hot oven and bake for 15-20 minutes. Leave to stand out of the oven for 4-5 minutes before serving.

Butter Bean Country Casserole

—◆—

This substantial dish is almost a meal in itself. All it needs is a bowl of salad and some fruit to finish. Chopped nuts can be substituted for the cheese – half quantities will be sufficient.

4 *small onions, peeled and sliced*
3 *tablespoons cooking oil*
350g *(12oz) mushrooms, sliced*
2 × 425g *(15oz) cans of butter*
  beans, drained

6-8 *tomatoes, chopped*
salt and freshly ground black
  pepper
125g *(4oz) cheddar cheese, grated*
125g *(4oz) breadcrumbs*

1. Fry the onions in the cooking oil until transparent. Add the sliced mushrooms and continue frying for 5-6 minutes.

2. Add beans and tomatoes to the onions and mushrooms. Season and heat through.

3. Place in an ovenproof dish and sprinkle with grated cheese and breadcrumbs. Brown under the grill and serve at once.

African Curried Vegetables
—◆—

Peanuts, or groundnuts as they are often called, crop up in all kinds of African dishes. Here peanut butter gives a lovely smoothness to the sauce.

1 *onion, peeled and chopped*
2 *garlic cloves, peeled and crushed*
2 *teaspoons freshly grated root*
  ginger
2 *tablespoons cooking oil*
4 *cardamom pods, slightly crushed*
2 *cloves*
1 *tablespoon ground coriander*
1 *teaspoon ground cumin*

1 *teaspoon curry powder*
450g *(1lb) mixed vegetables*
  (cauliflower, carrots and
  potatoes)
600ml *(1 pint) water*
1 *heaped tablespoon peanut butter*
salt and freshly ground black
  pepper

1. Fry the onion, garlic and ginger in the oil. Add the spices and continue cooking for 2-3 minutes.

2. Add the chopped vegetables and water, bring to the boil, cover and simmer for about 30-40 minutes.

3. Drain off the liquid and mix with the peanut butter. Return to pan and correct seasoning if necessary. Simmer for a further 5-10 minutes before serving.

Mixed Vegetables with Sunflower Seed Dumplings

——◆——

This American recipe from the Mid West is a dumpling lover's dream. The sunflower seeds give a nutty texture to the dumplings and the Tabasco adds a zing to the vegetables.

2 tablespoons oil
2 leeks, washed and sliced
1 large red pepper, seeded and cut into 1cm (1/2in) squares
2 tablespoons plain flour
1 × 400g (14oz) can of peeled tomatoes
150ml (1/4 pint) vegetable stock (see page xii)
450g (1lb) swede, peeled and cut into large dice
225g (8oz) parsnips, peeled and cut into large dice
a few drops of Tabasco sauce

225g (8oz) courgettes, trimmed and thickly sliced
300g (10oz) cup mushrooms, wiped and thickly sliced
salt and freshly ground black pepper

Dumplings
75g (3oz) margarine
175g (6oz) wholemeal self-raising flour
50g (2oz) sunflower seeds
a little cold water to mix

1. Heat the oil in a large saucepan and cook the leeks and red pepper over a gentle heat for 3 minutes. Stir in the flour and cook for a minute. Gradually stir in the tomatoes and the stock. Bring to the boil, stirring all the time.

2. Add the swede, parsnips and Tabasco, cover and simmer gently for 15 minutes, stirring occasionally.

3. Meanwhile, make the dumplings. Rub the margarine into the flour and stir in the sunflower seeds. Add just enough cold water to form a not too stiff dough. Shape into twelve balls.

4. Stir the courgettes, mushrooms and seasoning into the simmered vegetables and top with the dumplings. Cover and cook over a gentle heat for a further 20 minutes.

100

Aloo Gobi

—◆—

I serve this cauliflower and potato curry with Tarka Dhal (see page 97), rice and lots of poppadums. The best way to cook the latter is in the microwave. They take about 1 minute on full power and come out crisp and not at all fatty.

1 tablespoon cooking oil
1/4 teaspoon whole coriander seeds
1/8 teaspoon cumin seeds
2-3 cloves
2 baby cauliflowers, or 1/2 medium
   cauliflower, broken into florets
350g (12oz) potatoes, peeled and
   cut into large dice

1 teaspoon each of ground cumin
   and ground coriander
1/2 teaspoon turmeric
1 small green chilli, seeded and
   finely chopped (optional)
salt and freshly ground black
   pepper
8 tablespoons plain yoghurt

1. Heat the oil in a small heavy pan and fry the coriander and cumin seeds and cloves over a high heat until they begin to pop – about 1/2-3/4 minute.

2. Add all the remaining ingredients and bring to the boil. Cover and simmer for 15-20 minutes until the vegetables are tender and the juices fairly thick and creamy.

Fennel Bean Pot

—◆—

Fennel seed are worth seeking out for this unusual bean pot. It is also worth the trouble of using dried rather than canned beans. The longer cooking time allows all the flavours to marry up into a delicious whole.

75g (3oz) dried haricot beans
75g (3oz) dried black-eye beans
50g (2oz) dried butter beans
2 onions, peeled and chopped
2 garlic cloves, peeled and chopped
1 tablespoon cooking oil

$^1/_2$ teaspoon fennel seeds
2 tablespoons freshly chopped
  chervil or parsley
salt and freshly ground black
  pepper
300ml ($^1/_2$ pint) red wine

1. Soak the beans in cold water overnight.

2. Preheat the oven to 190°C/375°F/Gas 5.

3. Fry the onion and garlic in the cooking oil until golden. Add the beans along with the fennel seeds, chervil and seasoning.

4. Transfer to an earthenware casserole dish and pour on the red wine. Cover and bake for 1$^1/_2$ hours.

5. Increase the temperature to 200°C/400°F/Gas 6 and bake for a further 40-45 minutes. Stir from time to time.

EGG AND CHEESE DISHES

———◆———

These dishes have eggs and/or cheese as their major ingredient. They should be served with one or two vegetable dishes, or perhaps a salad and potatoes.

There is quite a selection of vegetarian cheeses, made without rennet, available now in the shops (see page xi). However, most of them tend to be English, and it is difficult to find vegetarian equivalents of Italian and French cheeses. If you don't want to use those rennet-based cheeses which I have included for their flavour, talk to your cheesemonger about suitable substitutes.

Marinated Brie can be served as a starter or indeed a final course, or with a large main-course salad. Smaller versions of Cheese Nut Patties are a welcome part of a canapé buffet, and individual Sun-Dried Tomato Quiches and Pepper and Olive Tartlets can also be served on a hot or cold buffet.

Marinated Brie

———◆———

Any soft cheese with a rind works well in this recipe. The cheese seems to take up the flavours, particularly of the oil (which must be extra virgin, the best grade of olive oil). Serve with mixed salad as an interesting variation on the cheese salad theme, or as a cheese course instead of a dessert.

150ml (¹/₄ pint) extra virgin olive
  oil
12 black peppercorns
2 garlic cloves, peeled and chopped

1 teaspoon dried mixed herbs
350g (12oz) Brie, cut into slices
a little salt to taste

1. Heat the oil in a small pan with the peppercorns, garlic and herbs. When the mixture starts to bubble, remove from the heat and leave to cool.

2. Arrange the slices of Brie in a shallow dish. Add a little salt to the cooked oil and spoon over the cheese. Leave to stand for at least 4 hours before serving.

Gratin of Kohlrabi

—◆—

Though less well known here, kohlrabi has long been a favourite vegetable in Germany. This dish makes a rich but unusual starter, or it may be served as a vegetable accompaniment to a casserole or bake.

4 kohlrabi, peeled and sliced
salt and freshly ground black
 pepper

150ml (¹/₄ pint) double cream
2 egg yolks

1. Cook the kohlrabi in a very little salted boiling water until just tender. Drain, retaining the cooking liquor. Place the kohlrabi slices in four individual heatproof dishes and keep warm.

2. Bring the cooking liquor to the boil again and continue boiling until it is reduced to about 3 tablespoons.

3. Lightly whisk the cream and whisk in the egg yolks. Pour this mixture into the vegetable liquid and heat gently, whisking all the time. Do not allow the mixture to boil. When the mixture begins to thicken a little, pour it over the kohlrabi.

4. Place the dishes under a hot grill until a thin golden skin forms on the surface. Serve at once.

Celery Cheese Gratin

—◆—

Serve this unusual celery dish — which has a light but crunchy texture — for lunch or supper, with potatoes and another vegetable.

1 small head of celery
2 tablespoons milk
175g (6oz) Cheddar cheese, grated
2 eggs, beaten

celery salt
freshly ground black pepper
50g (2oz) fresh wholemeal
*   breadcrumbs*

1. Preheat the oven to 190°C/350°F/Gas 5.

2. Wash the celery and grate on a medium grater. Place in a saucepan with the milk. Bring to the boil and simmer gently for about 15-20 minutes until the celery is tender. Stir from time to time. Leave to cool.

3. Mix with the cheese, egg, celery salt and black pepper. Spoon into a greased pie dish, cover with breadcrumbs and bake for 30-35 minutes.

Italian Potato and Pecorino Pie

—◆—

I serve this dish with a mass of grilled tomatoes topped with a little pesto sauce (see pages 48-49). If you cannot find Pecorino cheese, use any well-flavoured mature hard cheese.

1kg (2lb) potatoes, peeled
1 bunch of spring onions, sliced
1 garlic clove, peeled and crushed
225g (8oz) aged Pecorino Sardo,
*   grated*

4 eggs, beaten
250ml (8fl oz) plain yoghurt
salt and freshly ground black
*   pepper*

1. Preheat the oven to 200°C/400°F/Gas 6.

2. Grate the potatoes into a colander and squeeze thoroughly with a paper towel to remove all the water.

3. Mix with all the remaining ingredients and spoon into a greased shallow baking dish. Bake for 1 hour, until crispy on top.

Cheese Nut Patties

It's worth cooking the potatoes from scratch for these flavourful and interestingly textured patties. *Tofu* can be used in place of cottage cheese.

MAKES 8

700g (1¹/₂lb) potatoes, scrubbed
350g (12oz) cottage cheese
75g (3oz) shelled peanuts, ground
2 tablespoons chopped fresh chives
    or spring onions

salt and freshly ground black
    pepper
50g (2oz) fresh breadcrumbs,
    toasted
cooking oil to shallow fry

1. Cook the potatoes in boiling salted water until tender, then peel. Mash with the cottage cheese and ground nuts.

2. Add the chives or spring onions and some seasoning. Mix well.

3. Divide the mixture into eight portions and shape into balls. Roll in breadcrumbs until coated all over and flatten into patties.

4. Shallow fry on both sides until golden, about 4-5 minutes in total.

Potato and Mushroom Celeste

Instead of Brie I sometimes use Camembert in this dish for a stronger flavour. Take care if you do the same; because it is served hot, the taste can be a bit overwhelming – particularly if the cheese is too ripe.

700g (1¹/₂lb) potatoes, peeled and
    sliced
3 onions, peeled and sliced
4 tomatoes, skinned (see page xiii)
    and sliced
225g (8oz) mushrooms, sliced

225g (8oz) Brie cheese, sliced
1 teaspoon summer savory
¹/₂ teaspoon garlic salt
salt and freshly ground black
    pepper
150ml (¹/₄ pint) double cream

1. Preheat the oven to 200°C/400°F/Gas 6..

2. Layer the vegetables and cheese in a casserole dish, sprinkling each layer with herbs and seasonings. Finish with a layer of potatoes.

3. Pour the cream over the top, cover and bake for about 45 minutes.

Individual Sun-Dried Tomato Quiches

——◆——

These quiches are so good that I make six and serve four as a main course and use the remaining two for packed lunches the next day. I use half quantity of the pastry recipe given on page 148 for Pâtes de Béziers, but you can use any kind of shortcrust pastry, including ready-made or frozen.

MAKES 6

225g (8oz) shortcrust pastry
15g (1/2oz) sun-dried tomatoes
boiling water
2 eggs, beaten

50g (2oz) Parmesan cheese, grated
4 tablespoons plain yoghurt
salt and freshly ground black
  pepper

1. Preheat the oven to 190°C/375°F/Gas 5.

2. Roll out the pastry and use to line six 10cm (4in) tartlet tins. Leave in the fridge until required.

3. Pour sufficient boiling water over the tomatoes to just cover them and leave to stand for 15 minutes. Drain and slice thinly.

4. Mix the eggs with the cheese and yoghurt, and stir in the tomato strips and seasoning. Spoon into the pastry cases and bake for 25-30 minutes.

Pepper and Olive Tartlets

— ◆ —

This variation on the quiche theme uses *fromage frais* – a skimmed-milk soft cheese. Silken *tofu* can be substituted for the *fromage frais*. Red peppers give the sweetest flavour but green ones can also be used.

MAKES 6

225g (8oz) shortcrust pastry
(450g) 1lb red peppers, seeded and
  quartered
1 egg

125g (4oz) fromage frais or quark
salt and freshly ground black
  pepper
12 black olives, pitted

1. Preheat the oven to 190°C/375°F/Gas 5.

2. Roll out the pastry and use to line six 10cm (4in) tartlet tins.

3. Place the pieces of red pepper, skin up, on a grill tray and place under a high heat until lightly seared all over. Remove to a bowl and cover with a lid. Leave to stand for 10-15 minutes, then peel and discard the skin. Cut into strips.

4. Beat the egg with the *fromage frais*, and stir in the peppers and seasoning. Spoon into the prepared pastry cases, dot with olives, and bake for 35 minutes. Serve warm or cold.

Cauliflower Soufflé

— ◆ —

Cauliflower purée takes the place of the traditional roux sauce in this recipe, and so it is very quick and easy to make.

1 medium cauliflower
3 eggs, separated

salt and freshly ground black
  pepper

1. Preheat the oven to 200°C/400°F/Gas 6 and grease four individual soufflé dishes.

2. Steam the cauliflower until soft, then rub through a sieve. Leave to cool.

3. Mix the egg yolks with the cauliflower purée and seasoning.

4. Whisk the egg whites until stiff, and fold into the cauliflower mixture.

5. Pour into four individual soufflé dishes and bake for 10-15 minutes until set and slightly brown on top.

Chive and Tomato Soufflé

Tomatoes and chives are a winning combination whatever time of year, but the flavours always remind me of summer. To make individual soufflés, divide the mixture between 6-8 ramekins (depending on size) and bake for 20 minutes.

300ml (¹/₂ pint) milk
1 tablespoon tomato purée
75g (3oz) butter
50g (2oz) flour
4 whole eggs separated, plus 1
*   extra egg white*

50g (2oz) hard cheese, grated
bunch of fresh chives, chopped
75g (3oz) tomatoes, peeled and
*   chopped*

1. Preheat the oven to 190°C/375°F/Gas 5.

2. Mix together the milk and tomato purée. Melt the butter in a saucepan. Add the flour and cook for a minute.

3. Gradually add the milk and tomato mixture and bring to the boil, stirring all the time. Cook for 3 minutes.

4. Remove from the heat and beat in the egg yolks, then stir in the cheese, chives and chopped tomatoes.

5. Whisk the egg whites until stiff and stir a couple of tablespoons into the soufflé mixture. Fold in the rest of the egg whites then spoon into a greased 1.25 litre (2¹/₄ pint) soufflé dish.

6. Bake for 45-50 minutes until golden brown and set in the centre. Serve at once.

South American Baked Eggs

——◆——

This variation on eggs in potato nests has masses of flavour, and makes a good snack or light supper dish. Serve with a tossed green salad and crusty rolls.

4 onions, peeled and chopped
1 green pepper, seeded and
  chopped
2 tablespoons cooking oil
1 × 400g (14oz) can of red kidney
  beans, drained

1 teaspoon dried thyme
salt and freshly ground black
  pepper
4 large eggs
4 tablespoons red wine

1. Preheat the oven to 220°C/425°F/Gas 7.

2. Fry the onion and pepper in the cooking oil to soften.

3. Mash the beans with a fork and add to the onions with the thyme and seasoning. Mix well and spoon into an ovenproof dish.

4. Make four wells in the mixture and break an egg into each one. Pour the wine over the top and bake for about 15-20 minutes until the eggs are set to your liking.

Grated Vegetable Rösti

——◆——

There is no need to pre-cook the potatoes for this variation on the Swiss speciality. Different vegetables, such as grated celeriac or parsnips, can be added to the potato base in place of carrots and celery. Serve with spinach or beans to make a satisfying meal.

2 large potatoes, peeled
1 large carrot, peeled and grated
3 celery sticks, sliced very thinly
1 onion, peeled and grated

3 large eggs, beaten
salt and freshly ground black
  pepper
2 tablespoons cooking oil

1. Grate the potatoes *after* preparing the carrots, celery and onion, as they have a tendency to discolour. Place the grated vegetables in a colander and squeeze out all the water from the vegetables by pressing with kitchen paper. Mix the vegetables with the eggs and seasoning.

2. Heat the oil in a 20cm (8in) frying pan and spoon the vegetable mixture into it. Spread out to cover the base of the pan and turn the heat down. Cook slowly for about 15-20 minutes until well browned underneath. Turn the mixture over with a fish slice and cook on the other side for a further 10-15 minutes.

Polenta Stuffed Peppers
—◆—

Popular in Italy, polenta or yellow cornmeal is used to make dumplings or served as an accompaniment to other dishes. This unusual recipe from a Romanian friend uses it to stuff multi-coloured peppers.

4 medium peppers of different colours	*25g (1oz) butter*
400ml (14fl oz) water	*75g (3oz) Parmesan or any really hard cheese, grated*
1 teaspoon salt	*freshly ground black pepper*
75g (3oz) polenta	*3 eggs*

1. Preheat the oven to 180°C/350°F/Gas 4.

2. Cut the stalk ends off the peppers and scoop out all the centre membranes and seeds. Place on an ovenproof plate and bake for 10 minutes. Remove from the oven.

2. Meanwhile, pour the water, salt and polenta into a heavy-based pan. Slowly bring to the boil, stirring continuously. Continue cooking gently, still stirring frequently for about 15-20 minutes until the polenta is fairly thick.

3. Remove from the heat and beat in the butter, cheese, black pepper and eggs, one at a time.

4. Spoon this mixture into the hot peppers and bake for 40 minutes.

Broad Bean and Herb Omelette

——◆——

Broad beans seem to go very well with eggs, and here they are used to fill an omelette. This recipe is sufficient for two people, so double up for four.

SERVES 2

125g (4oz) podded broad beans
2 tablespoons freshly chopped
  parsley
2 teaspoons freshly chopped chives
1 teaspoon freshly chopped
  summer savory or oregano

4 eggs
2 tablespoons water
salt and freshly ground black
  pepper
a knob of butter

1. Cook the broad beans in lightly salted boiling water for about 10-15 minutes until tender. Drain well and mix with the herbs.

2. Beat the eggs, water and seasoning together with a fork. Melt the butter in an omelette pan and when hot pour in the egg mixture. Stir lightly two or three times only. Cook until just set.

3. Place the bean and herb mixture over one half of the omelette and fold the other half over it. Serve at once.

Vietnamese Egg Pancakes
—◆—

I first had these spicy filled pancakes in a Vietnamese restaurant in the south of France. They fall somewhere between a flat omelette and a crispy pancake. This quantity makes quite a filling main course.

Pancakes
600ml (1 pint) boiling water
200g (7oz) desiccated coconut
1 small onion, peeled and very
    thinly sliced
cooking oil
a pinch of whole cumin seeds
75g (3oz) rice or potato flour
25g (1oz) wholemeal flour, sieved
¹/₄ teaspoon turmeric
3 large eggs, beaten

Filling
1 large garlic clove, peeled and
    crushed
1 tablespoon freshly grated root
    ginger
6 spring onions, sliced lengthways
3-4 tablespoons olive oil
175g (6oz) button mushrooms,
    thickly sliced
225g (8oz) mangetout, cut into
    strips
225g (8oz) beansprouts
1 tablespoon soy sauce (optional)

1. Start the pancakes by pouring the boiling water over the coconut. Leave to stand for about 20-30 minutes. Squeeze out the liquid from the coconut to give 300ml (¹/₂ pint) coconut milk.

2. Fry the onion in 1 tablespoon of the cooking oil with the cumin seeds until well browned.

3. Mix the two flours with the turmeric, then stir in the eggs, coconut milk and fried onion and cumin seeds.

4. Heat a very little cooking oil in a 30cm (12in) non-stick frying pan, and spoon a quarter of the pancake mixture into the pan. Tilt and roll the pan until the mixture is spread out well. Cook until well browned and slightly crisp underneath, then turn over and cook the other side until also brown and slightly crisp. Remove and keep warm. Make three more pancakes in the same way and keep warm.

5. For the filling, stir-fry the garlic, ginger and spring onions in the olive oil. Add the mushrooms and stir-fry for another minute, then add the mangetout, followed by the beansprouts, and soy sauce if using – taking about 2¹/₂-3 minutes in all.

6. Spoon on to the pancakes and fold over. Serve at once.

113

SALADS

—◆—

These salads are very versatile and varied. They can be served as a first course, or as an accompaniment to the main course. Some, like Chicory Salad and Fresh Lentil and Radish Salad, make main-course dishes in their own right.

Most salads benefit from a good dressing, which may be based on oil and vinegar, oil and lemon juice, yoghurt, *tofu* or cheese. I personally think the best oil to use for salads is olive oil. If you're not sure about the flavour, try a plain olive oil first, and then move on to the fuller flavoured virgin and extra virgin oils. Incidentally, the words 'cold-pressed' or 'first-pressing' are now merely hype. With the advent of hydraulic presses throughout the olive oil producing areas, all of these grades of oil come from a single pressing. The classification thereafter depends on the acidity level, aroma, colour and flavour.

Tofu Dressing for Mixed Green Salad

—◆—

This easy-to-make dressing can be flavoured in lots of different ways. Simply add your chosen flavouring to the mixture in the blender. You may need to add a little water if using fresh *tofu*. This dressing can be stored in the fridge for 2-3 days.

175g (6oz) tofu *(fresh or silken)*
2 tablespoons lemon juice or wine
  vinegar

2 tablespoons salad oil
salt and freshly ground black
  pepper

1. Purée all the ingredients in a blender or food processor, or mash with a fork and mix with a wire whisk. Stir in your chosen flavourings.

Suggested flavourings

3 tablespoons chopped spring onions and parsley *or*
1 teaspoon curry powder mixed with 1 tablespoon mild chutney *or*
1 tablespoon peanut butter or *tahina* paste

Sala Beetroot Salad

—◆—

This mixture, derived from a more elaborate salad encountered when staying with a family in Finland, makes an excellent side salad for a lasagne, a Pasticcio (macaroni and aubergine pie, see page 53), and other pasta dishes.

225g (8oz) cooked beetroot, peeled and diced
1 large sweet/sour pickled cucumber, diced
a little grated orange rind

1/2 bunch of watercress

Dressing
2 tablespoons walnut oil
freshly ground black pepper

1. Toss together the beetroot, cucumber and orange rind and spoon on to a bed of watercress.

2. Just before serving, drizzle over the oil and sprinkle with pepper.

Cauliflower Salad

—◆—

Cauliflower is very good eaten raw. Try small florets as dippers for Guacamole (see page 161) or use them in this crunchy winter salad.

1/2 cauliflower, cut into small florets
1 × 200g (7oz) can of red pimentos, drained and finely chopped
7.5cm (3in) cucumber, diced

1 green apple, cored and diced
1 tablespoon flaked almonds

Dressing
3 tablespoons salad oil
1 tablespoon white wine vinegar

1. Place all the salad ingredients in a bowl and toss lightly together.

2. Mix the oil and vinegar and pour over the top. Chill for half an hour. Toss again and serve.

facing page 114: Mixed Vegetables with Sunflower Seed Dumplings (page 100)

opposite: Chive and Tomato Soufflé (page 109)

Aubergine Salad

———◆———

This fine textured and flavoured recipe originates in the Middle East where it is usually served with hot pitta bread.

2 aubergines
1/2 green pepper, seeded and finely chopped
2 tomatoes, skinned (see page 00) seeded and chopped
1/2 small onion, peeled and finely chopped
1 garlic clove, peeled and crushed

1 teaspoon ground cumin
1 tablespoon freshly chopped parsley
2 teaspoons olive oil
juice of 1 lemon
salt and freshly ground black pepper

1. Preheat the oven to 200°C/400°F/Gas 6.

2. Bake the aubergines in their skins until they feel soft to the touch and the skins have turned black (about an hour). Leave to cool.

3. Cut open the aubergine and scrape out all the flesh. Discard the skin and finely chop the flesh. Mix with all the remaining ingredients, seasoning to taste. Serve garnished with a little more chopped parsley.

Carrot and Fennel Coleslaw

———◆———

Cabbage is, of course, the usual base for coleslaw but there is no reason why other vegetables should not be used in the same way. Here is an idea that I worked out while in France one summer. I experimented with lovely long thin new carrots from a local market but any carrots will do.

3 carrots, peeled and cut into long thin sticks
1 head of fennel, very finely sliced

3 tablespoons mayonnaise
1/2 teaspoon Dijon mustard
freshly ground black pepper

1. Blanch the carrot and fennel for 3 minutes in boiling water and then plunge into cold water for the same amount of time. Drain well.

2. Mix the mayonnaise with the mustard and pepper and toss with the completely cooled vegetables. Store in the fridge until required.

Broccoli Salad

—◆—

Take care not to overcook the broccoli for this salad. If you do it will be mushy and unpleasant. The dressing is quite substantial, and full of flavour.

450g (1lb) large broccoli or
  calabrese heads

Dressing
1 hard-boiled egg, shelled and
  chopped
1 tomato, skinned (see page xiii)
  seeded and chopped
1 small sweet/sour pickled
  cucumber, finely chopped

4 spring onions, finely chopped
6 tablespoons olive oil
2 tablespoons cider or white wine
  vinegar
freshly ground black pepper
1 teaspoon freshly chopped
  tarragon, or 1/4 teaspoon dried
  tarragon

1. Steam the broccoli in a steamer, or boil in a very little boiling salted water. Drain and leave to cool.

2. Mix the chopped egg, tomato, cucumber and spring onion in a small basin.

3. Mix the oil with the remaining ingredients and beat well, then mix with the egg and tomato mixture. Chill in the fridge.

4. Arrange the pieces of broccoli on four small serving plates. Pour the dressing over the top and serve.

Marinated Mushroom and Avocado Salad

—◆—

A ripe avocado will yield slightly to gentle pressure. Unripe avocados will ripen in the fruit bowl in a couple of days. Choose only really ripe avocados for this salad and mix in at the last minute. Serve on a bed of mixed salad leaves or with Chinese beansprouts.

225g (8oz) small button mushrooms, quartered
75ml (3fl oz) olive oil
25ml (1fl oz) fresh lemon juice
1 teaspoon tomato purée
1/4 teaspoon dried thyme
a pinch of fennel seeds
salt and freshly ground black pepper

75g (3oz) cashew nuts
1/4 green pepper, seeded and finely chopped
2 spring onions, finely chopped
2 teaspoons freshly chopped basil
a pinch of grated lemon rind
1 large or 2 small avocados, peeled, stoned and chopped
sprigs of continental parsley

1. Mix the mushrooms with the olive oil, lemon juice, tomato purée, herbs and seasoning and leave to stand for at least an hour. Stir from time to time.

2. Meanwhile dry-fry the cashew nuts in a hot frying pan. Keep the nuts on the move or they will burn. Cool.

3. Just before serving add the nuts and all the remaining ingredients except the parsley to the marinated mushrooms. Toss well together and serve garnished with the parsley.

Cauliflower and Grilled Red Pepper Salad

——◆——

This can be served very successfully either as part of a cold buffet or as a first course. The idea comes from Italy where they use far more capers in their cooking than we do in the UK.

SERVES 8-10

1 cauliflower
4 red peppers, seeded and cut into quarters
8 sprigs of fresh tarragon
8 large fresh sprigs of continental parsley
40 black olives, stoned and quartered

3 tablespoons capers, drained

Dressing
6 tablespoons extra virgin olive oil
1 tablespoon red wine vinegar
salt and freshly ground black pepper
1/4 garlic clove, peeled and crushed

1. Steam the cauliflower for 4-5 minutes; it should still have quite a lot of bite to it. Cover and leave to cool, then break into florets.

2. Grill the peppers skin side up, until the skins blacken. Place in a bowl, cover with a plate, and leave to cool. Peel off and discard the skin, and cut the flesh into strips.

3. Chop one large sprig of the tarragon and mix together with all the dressing ingredients. Leave to stand until required.

4. Arrange the continental parsley on the serving plate and place strips of peppers on top. Dot with cauliflower florets and sprinkle with olives and capers. Spoon the dressing over the top and top with the remaining sprigs of tarragon. Serve at once.

119

Mixed Leaf and Pistachio Nut Salad

—◆—

Toasting nuts under the grill or in a hot dry frying pan seems to add an extra dimension to their flavour, but take care not to burn them. Keep an eye on them and turn constantly – they don't take long.

5-6 pieces of sun-dried tomato
1 bunch of watercress
mixed salad leaves
3 tablespoons shelled pistachio
  nuts, toasted
3 tablespoons pine kernels, toasted
8 baby artichoke hearts in oil
  (optional)

16 black olives
sprigs of fresh herbs

Dressing
6 tablespoons extra virgin olive oil
1 tablespoon orange or tarragon
  vinegar
salt and freshly ground black
  pepper

1. Soak the tomato in boiling water for 15-20 minutes. Drain and cut into strips.

2. Mix the watercress and salad leaves, and strew leaves over four plates. Sprinkle with nuts, pine kernels and tomato strips. Dot with artichokes (if using), olives and sprigs of herbs.

3. Beat the dressing ingredients together with a fork and spoon on at the last minute.

Bitter Salad with Grilled Red Peppers

—◆—

Choose two or three different leaves for this piquant Italian salad.

1 large or two small red peppers,
  seeded and quartered
mixed bitter leaves such as rocket
  or arugula, French dandelion,
  watercress and sorrel
6-10 black olives, halved
1 teaspoon capers, drained

Dressing
6 tablespoons extra virgin olive oil
1 tablespoon balsamic or sherry
  vinegar
salt and freshly ground black
  pepper

1. Place pepper pieces skin side up under a hot grill and leave until they begin to blacken. Place in a bowl and cover with a plate. Leave to cool. Remove and discard the skin and cut the flesh into strips.

2. Arrange the bitter leaves on four serving plates. Top with the pepper strips and sprinkle with the olives and capers.

3. Mix the dressing ingredients and pour over the top just before serving.

Warm Beansprout Salad with Feta Cheese

Warming the dressing brings out the full flavour of the olive oil, so choose a good one. Add the dressing at the last minute or the beansprouts will lose their crunch.

175g (6oz) Chinese beansprouts
1/2 small iceberg lettuce, shredded
12 small black olives
2 tablespoons salted peanuts
125g (4oz) Feta cheese, crumbled
a pinch of dried oregano

freshly ground black pepper

Dressing
1 tablespoon olive oil
1 tablespoon lemon juice

1. Toss the beansprouts in a bowl with the shredded lettuce. Sprinkle with olives and nuts.

2. For the dressing, mix the olive oil and lemon juice, and heat in a saucepan. Pour over the top of the sprouts.

3. Sprinkle the salad with Feta cheese and then with oregano and black pepper.

121

French Dandelion Salad with Chickpeas

—◆—

French dandelion is very similar to arugula or rocket, which can be used instead. French dandelion for my salad comes from my father's garden!

SERVES 2

3-4 sun-dried tomatoes
175g (6oz) canned chickpeas, drained
sprigs of fresh parsley and tarragon
50g (2oz) French dandelion
a few fresh sorrel leaves
4-5 clusters of lamb's lettuce
sprigs of fresh herbs

Dressing
4 tablespoons extra virgin olive oil
2 teaspoons lemon juice
a little grated lemon rind
2 tablespoons freshly chopped parsley
2 teaspoons freshly chopped tarragon
salt and freshly ground black pepper

1. Cover the tomatoes with boiling water and leave to stand for 15-20 minutes.

2. Mix all the dressing ingredients together and keep on one side.

3. Place the chickpeas in a bowl and cover with the dressing. Leave to stand until required.

4. Toss the parsley, tarragon and salad leaves together, and arrange on serving plates. Spoon the chickpeas and dressing over the top.

5. Drain the tomatoes and cut into strips. Arrange with sprigs of fresh herbs over the top of the salad and serve at once.

Chicory Salad

—◆—

I find that, with the eggs and cheese, this salad make a real midday meal in itself. But if you think you will be hungry add a home-made roll (see page 128).

100g (4oz) frozen peas
salt
4 heads of chicory, sliced into
    circles
3 hard-boiled eggs, shelled and
    chopped
100g (4oz) Cheddar cheese, diced

freshly ground black pepper
1 bunch of watercress

Dressing
2 tablespoons mayonnaise
1 teaspoon lemon juice
a pinch of dried mixed herbs

1. Cook the peas in lightly salted boiling water for 8 minutes. Drain and rinse under the cold tap. Leave to cool in a sieve.

2. Mix the chicory slices with the eggs, cheese and cold peas and season with black pepper.

3. Mix all the dressing ingredients together and add to the chicory mixture. Toss well and pile into the centre of a serving dish. Surround with sprigs of watercress.

Italian Panzanella Salad

This bread-based salad comes from Tuscany where the locals serve it at any time of the day, from a mid-morning snack to a late supper. Do be sure to break the bread up into small pieces.

4 thick slices of Italian bread
4 tablespoons water
1 tablespoon red wine vinegar
2 large bunches of basil, coarsely chopped
1 small bunch of continental parsley, coarsely chopped

1 cucumber, diced
450g (1lb) tomatoes, seeded and diced
6-8 tablespoons extra virgin olive oil
sprigs of basil

1. Place the slices of bread in a dish and pour over the water and vinegar. Leave to stand for 30 minutes. Squeeze the bread dry, break up with a fork and put into a bowl.

2. Add all the remaining ingredients except for the oil and basil sprigs. Toss well together.

3. Just before serving, add the olive oil and serve at once, garnished with sprigs of basil.

French Lentil and Radish Salad

—◆—

The lentils can be cooked in advance and kept in the fridge until required. I like to cook double quantities of lentils and use half for this salad and the rest as extra garnish to other salads later in the week.

225g (8oz) whole dried green or
* brown lentils*
1 onion, peeled and stuck with
* 2 cloves*
1 small carrot, peeled
1 bouquet garni
2 tablespoons olive oil
1 teaspoon cider vinegar
1 tablespoon freshly chopped
* parsley*
1 teaspoon freshly chopped
* tarragon, chives or dill*

4 small spring onions, finely
* chopped*
salt and freshly ground black
* pepper*
5cm (2in) cucumber, sliced
¹/₂ bunch of radishes, trimmed and
* sliced*
¹/₂ green pepper, seeded and sliced
sprigs of fresh herbs (tarragon,
* chives and parsley)*

1. Wash the lentils in cold water. Place in a saucepan with the onion, carrot and *bouquet garni*. Cover with water and bring to the boil. Reduce the heat and simmer for 30 minutes until just tender. The lentils should retain their shape and a little of their bite. Drain.

2. Mix the lentils with the oil, vinegar, fresh herbs, spring onions and seasoning. Leave to cool.

3. Add the cucumber, radishes and green pepper just before serving, and pile on to individual plates. Garnish with sprigs of fresh herbs.

Special Occasion and Party Food

DINNERS

If I am planning to entertain I am usually prepared to spend just a little longer than usual in the kitchen. Accordingly I have included some of my more elaborate favourites in this section.

However, I must say that I rarely do more than one complicated dish even when I am entertaining, and dishes such as Vegetable Terrine or Baked Courgette Moulds would be followed by some of the quick-to-prepare pasta or stir-fry dishes. Carrot Coulibiac, or Red Pepper Gougère, Ratatouille Roulade or Asparagus Pancake Stack might be preceded by pre-prepared soups, interesting salad starters such as Cauliflower and Grilled Red Pepper Salad or a quickly made hot starter such as Love Apples or Venetian-Style Courgettes.

Complete the meal with a fresh fruit salad or an interesting cheese board.

Wholemeal Rolls

This is my father's excellent recipe for crusty wholemeal rolls.

MAKES 10-12

450g (1lb) wholemeal flour *1 teaspoon salt*
15g (¹/₂oz) activated dried yeast *375ml (13fl oz) lukewarm water*

1. Mix the flour, yeast and salt in a large bowl. Make a well in the centre and pour in the water. Mix to a soft (slightly sticky) dough.

2. Turn on to a floured surface and knead for 10 minutes. Shape into rolls and place on a greased baking tray. Leave in a warm place to rise to double their size – about an hour.

3. Preheat the oven to 230°C/450°F/Gas 8.

4. Bake the risen rolls for 10-12 minutes. Test to see if the rolls are ready by tapping with your fingernails. They should sound hollow.

Herb and Lemon Bread

—◆—

This is a delicious variation on the popular garlic bread. It goes very well with delicately flavoured salads, stir-fry dishes or pasta.

SERVES 4-6

75g (3oz) butter, softened
2 tablespoons freshly chopped
 parsley
1 tablespoon freshly chopped
 chervil

1 tablespoon freshly chopped basil
a few fresh thyme leaves
1 teaspoon finely grated lemon rind
freshly ground black pepper
1 French baguette

1. Preheat the oven to 230°C/450°F/Gas 8.

2. Mix the butter, herbs, lemon rind and pepper to a soft paste.

3. Slice the *baguette* into thick chunks. Butter each slice with the herb mixture and press back into a loaf shape. Wrap in foil and bake for about 5-8 minutes until crisp. Serve at once.

Winter variation

If fresh herbs are not easily available use ½ teaspoon mixed dried herbs, ½ teaspoon dried thyme and ¼ teaspoon dried rosemary instead.

Stuffed Pepper Rings
—◆—

You can vary the flavour of the stuffing by using different cheeses or by adding chopped herbs. Serve as a first course or on a cold buffet.

SERVES 6-8

4 medium green peppers	*125g (4oz) Cheddar cheese, grated*
225g (8oz) blue cheese, crumbled	*50g (2oz) walnuts, chopped*
300g (10oz) cream cheese	*freshly ground black pepper*

1. Cut the heads off the top of the peppers and scrape out the seeds and membranes.

2. Mix all the remaining ingredients together and stuff into the hollow peppers, pressing well down. Place in the fridge and chill until the stuffing is firm.

3. To serve, cut the peppers horizontally into slices.

Venetian-Style Courgettes
—◆—

This unusual Italian dish makes a very good first course for dinner parties. Prepare all the ingredients and quickly cook as the guests sit down and your co-host serves the wine.

450g (1lb) courgettes, trimmed	*1 tablespoon double cream*
25g (1oz) butter	*1 tablespoon freshly chopped*
1 tablespoon olive oil	*parsley*
1 egg	*salt and freshly ground black*
25g (1oz) Parmesan cheese, freshly grated	*pepper*

1. Slice the courgettes lengthways. Cut each section into two or three thick sticks and halve.

2. Heat the butter and oil in a frying pan and gently fry the courgettes over a low heat for about 5 minutes to soften them. Do not allow them to brown.

130

3. Mix all the remaining ingredients, beat well and pour into the pan. Stir everything with a wooden spoon and as soon as the egg sets, serve with wholemeal rolls (see page 128).

Carrot and Spinach Gâteau

Cut this colourful savory gâteau just like a cake and serve in wedges. When I made this for a dinner party recently, I was unable to buy fresh spinach, so substituted some Middle Eastern greens I found at the local Greek grocer. It worked very well. It won't, however, work with frozen spinach.

SERVES 6

450g (1lb) carrots, peeled and
   sliced
6 tablespoons milk
25g (1oz) butter
8 eggs, beaten

¼ teaspoon dried tarragon
salt and freshly ground black
   pepper
175g (6oz) large spinach leaves,
   stalks removed

1. Preheat the oven to 190°C/375°F/Gas 5.

2. Cook the carrots in a little boiling water for about 10-12 minutes until tender. Drain really well and purée in a blender or food processor or mash well.

3. Heat the milk and butter in a pan. When the mixture boils add the eggs and scramble until cooked. Add the tarragon and season to taste.

4. Plunge the spinach leaves into boiling water for 1 minute. Refresh in cold water and use three-quarters to line a 16cm (6½in) loose-based cake tin.

5. Spoon half the egg mixture into the tin. Then add the carrot in one layer and top with the remaining egg. Cover with remaining spinach leaves and then with foil and bake for 30 minutes. Remove from the tin to serve.

Watercress Soufflé

—◆—

Soufflés really are not as difficult as many people think. The secret is to make sure that the soufflé is well cooked so that it will not flop as you bring it to the table or put your spoon in it. Serve as an impressive first course.

2 bunches of watercress
75g (3oz) butter
50g (2oz) plain flour
300ml (¹/₂ pint) milk
50g (2oz) Cheddar cheese, grated

¹/₂ teaspoon dry mustard
salt and freshly ground black
  pepper
4 eggs, separated

1. Preheat the oven to 190°C/375°F/Gas 5.

2. Blanch the watercress in boiling water for 3 minutes. Drain very well and chop finely.

3. Melt the butter in a pan and stir in the flour. Gradually add the milk, stirring all the time. Bring to the boil and add the cheese, mustard, seasoning and blanched watercress. Cook for 3 minutes.

4. Remove from the heat and beat in the egg yolks.

5. Whisk the egg whites until stiff. Mix a tablespoon of the whites into the soufflé mixture and then fold in the rest.

6. Spoon into a 1.2 litre (2 pint) soufflé dish and bake for 45 minutes until the soufflé is well risen, firm to the touch in the centre, and browning at the side. Serve at once.

Baked Courgette Moulds

—◆—

Serve these delicately flavoured vegetable moulds with a light tomato sauce.

1 onion, peeled and finely chopped
1 garlic clove, peeled and crushed
2 tablespoons olive oil
450g (1lb) courgettes, trimmed and diced
25g (1oz) bread, without the crusts

75ml (3fl oz) milk
1 tablespoon freshly chopped basil
1 teaspoon freshly chopped mint
salt and freshly ground black pepper
2 eggs, beaten

1. Preheat the oven to 180°C/350°F/Gas 4.

2. Fry the onion and garlic in the olive oil for a minute or two until transparent. Add the courgettes and continue frying over a gentle heat for about 15 minutes, stirring from time to time.

3. Mix the bread and milk with the herbs and seasoning, and leave to stand.

4. When the courgettes are cooked, mash the bread and milk well with a fork. Stir in the eggs and then the courgette mixture.

5. Spoon into individual ramekins or a large mould and place in a baking tin filled with 5cm (2in) hot water. Bake for 50-60 minutes until set through the centre.

Stuffed Vine Leaves

—◆—

This stuffing can also be used to stuff Chinese leaves or large spinach leaves. For these, cook in more tomato juice and less oil.

SERVES 6

1/2 small onion, peeled and very
    finely sliced
4 tablespoons olive oil
125g (4oz) long-grain rice
300ml (1/2 pint) water or vegetable
    stock (see page xii)
1 tablespoon raisins, chopped
2 tablespoons pine kernels

3 tablespoons freshly chopped
    parsley
1 teaspoon freshly chopped mint
juice of 1 lemon
salt and freshly ground black
    pepper
24 vine leaves
1 tablespoon tomato juice

1. Fry the onion in a tablespoon of the olive oil until soft. Add the rice and stir well. Pour on the water and add the raisins, pine kernels, parsley and mint. Bring to the boil, stir once and cover with a lid. Simmer for 12 minutes. Add the lemon juice and seasoning and keep on one side.

2. Meanwhile blanch the vine leaves by plunging into boiling water for 3 minutes, removing and plunging into cold water to stop the cooking process. Drain the leaves and cut off the stalks.

3. Place a small spoonful of the rice mixture on each leaf and roll up, tucking the ends in like a parcel.

4. Stack in a small pan. Add the remaining oil, the tomato juice and sufficient water to cover. Place a small saucer on top of the stuffed vine leaves so that they cannot float on the liquid, and weight it down. Cover and simmer for 45 minutes. Leave to cool without removing the lid. When serving, discard the liquid.

Stuffed Chinese Leaves

———◆———

This recipe was inspired by a Polish recipe for stuffed cabbage, and the ingredients seem to go well with the rather stronger flavour of Chinese leaves.

SERVES 4 at a dinner or 6 on a hot buffet table

1 head of Chinese leaves
50g (2oz) long-grain rice
3 tomatoes, skinned (see page xiii)
and chopped
50g (2oz) mixed nuts (almonds,
hazelnuts, walnuts), chopped
1 onion, peeled and finely chopped

3 tablespoons freshly chopped
parsley
salt and freshly ground black
pepper
600ml (1 pint) strongly flavoured
stock (see page xii)
juice of 1 lemon

1. Remove twelve of the large outer Chinese leaves and blanch by plunging into boiling water for 1 minute. Transfer to a bowl of cold water and drain.

2. Mix the rice, tomatoes, nuts, onions and parsley in a bowl and season. Place a tablespoon of the filling on each Chinese leaf and roll up neatly, taking care not to tear it.

3. Shred the remaining Chinese leaves and place in the base of a wide saucepan. Carefully arrange the stuffed leaves on top.

4. Mix the stock cube with the boiling water and pour over the top, with the lemon juice. Bring to the boil, cover and simmer gently for 30 minutes.

Mexican Layered Tostadas

——◆——

Tostadas are similar to taco shells, only flat. Buy them in packets in the Mexican speciality section at the supermarket. If you like your tomato sauce as hot as the Mexicans do, add more chilli.

2 tablespoons olive or cooking oil	**Sauce**
1 small onion, peeled and thinly sliced	1 tablespoon olive or cooking oil
1 × 435g (15^1/$_2$oz) can of red kidney beans, drained	1 large onion, peeled and sliced
salt and freshly ground black pepper	1 green pepper, seeded and chopped
1 × 125g (4oz) packet (12) tostada Shells	^{1}/$_2$ red pepper, seeded and chopped
100g (4oz) Cheddar cheese, grated	^{1}/$_2$-1 green chilli, seeded and finely chopped
6 lettuce leaves, shredded	1 × 400g (14oz) can of tomatoes
	1 tablespoon tomato purée
	^{1}/$_4$ teaspoon ground cumin
	a pinch of sugar

1. Preheat the oven to 190°C/350°F/Gas 4.

2. To make the sauce, heat one tablespoon of the oil in a pan and gently fry the onion, peppers and chilli for 3-4 minutes. Add all the remaining sauce ingredients. Bring the mixture to the boil and simmer for 45 minutes. Take off the lid and boil to reduce any excess liquid. The sauce should be quite thick.

3. For the bean mixture, heat the oil in a frying pan and fry the onion until well browned. Add the drained beans and seasoning, and mash with a potato masher. Cook for 2-3 minutes on one side until browned. Turn over and brown the other side. Keep warm.

4. Heat the tostada shells in the oven, as instructed on the packet. Place one on each of four individual plates and cover each with the fried beans. Add another tostada and cover with the sauce. Top with the remaining tostadas and sprinkle with grated cheese and shredded lettuce. Serve at once.

136

Vegetable Moussaka

—◆—

Greece supplies the original version of this deliciously filling vegetable dish. Serve on its own with salad.

SERVES 4-6

4 tablespoons cooking oil
2 large onions, peeled and sliced
4 large tomatoes, skinned (see page xiii) and chopped
1 tablespoon tomato purée
1/4 teaspoon dried thyme
1/2 teaspoon ground coriander
salt and freshly ground black pepper

125ml (4fl oz) vegetable stock (see page xii)
2 aubergines, sliced
700g (11/2lb) potatoes, peeled and sliced
50g (2oz) butter
50g (2oz) plain flour
450ml (3/4 pint) milk or soya milk
2 eggs, beaten

1. Preheat the oven to 200°C/400°F/Gas 6, and grease a large soufflé or casserole dish.

2. Heat 2 tablespoons of the cooking oil in a saucepan and fry the onions until lightly browned. Add the tomatoes, tomato purée, thyme, coriander and seasoning. Stir and add the stock or water. Bring to the boil, reduce the heat and simmer for 15-20 minutes.

3. Meanwhile, place the sliced aubergine in a shallow dish and sprinkle each slice with salt. Leave to stand for 15 minutes.

4. Parboil the sliced potatoes in a little salted water for about 8 minutes. Do not allow them to over-soften. Drain well.

5. Wash the aubergine slices under the tap and squeeze dry. Fry in the remaining cooking oil to brown lightly on each side.

6. Layer the tomato mixture with the potatoes and fried aubergine in the soufflé or casserole dish.

7. Heat the butter in a saucepan and stir in the flour. Next add the milk and bring to the boil, stirring all the time. Cook for 3 minutes. Remove from the heat and beat in the eggs. Season to taste.

8. Pour this sauce over the top of the moussaka, and bake in the centre of the oven for about 50-60 minutes, until the top is set and light brown in colour. Serve at once.

Carrot Coulibiac

—◆—

This vegetarian version of a Russian speciality can be made with parsnips or swede in place of carrot. It will taste good but it will not look anything like as colourful. If you use *tofu* in place of cheese you may need to add a little stock to moisten the mixture.

450g (1lb) carrots, peeled and grated
1 large onion, peeled and thinly sliced
25g (1oz) butter
1 tablespoon cooking oil
200g (7oz) quark low-fat soft cheese, or tofu
salt and freshly ground black pepper

75g (3oz) long-grain plain or brown rice
175ml (6fl oz) water
50g (2oz) frozen peas
1 × 370g (13oz) packet of frozen shortcrust or puff pastry, thawed
700g (1¹/₂lb) fresh spinach, or 1 × 225g (8oz) packet of leaf spinach, thawed
grated nutmeg

1. Preheat the oven to 200°C/400°F/Gas 6.

2. Gently fry the carrot and onion in the butter and oil for 6-8 minutes until soft. Do not allow the mixture to brown. Stir in the *quark* and seasoning.

3. Place the rice in a pan with the water and peas and bring to the boil. Reduce the heat, cover and simmer for 15 minutes until the rice is tender and all the liquid has been taken up. Remove from the heat and season to taste.

4. Cook and drain fresh spinach or drain frozen spinach.

5. Roll out the pastry to form a rectangle about 30 × 25cm (12 × 10in). Pile half the rice mixture down the centre. Carefully arrange half the spinach leaves over the top. Sprinkle with nutmeg, and spoon on the carrot mixture, then cover with the remaining spinach leaves and a little more nutmeg. Top with the rest of the rice mixture. Fold the pastry over the top and seal the join and ends with a little water.

6. Place join-side down on a greased baking tin and cook for 30-35 minutes until golden. Cut into slices to serve.

Tofu and Vegetable Satay

——◆——

The contrasting colours of the white *tofu* and fennel, the green ___ ___
and the black prunes, look most attractive. Serve on a bed of plain rice
with the sauce on the side. Creamed coconut comes in solid blocks that
have to be melted down to use. Look out for it in ethnic food shops.

225g (8oz) tofu, cut into 8 chunks
4 tablespoons cooking oil
1 tablespoon freshly grated root
* ginger*
4 spring onions, chopped
1 garlic clove, peeled and chopped
2 green peppers, seeded and
* quartered*
2 heads of fennel, trimmed and
* quartered*

8 no-soak prunes, stoned

Satay sauce
50g (2oz) creamed coconut
1 tablespoon soy sauce
1 tablespoon lemon juice
3 tablespoons peanut butter
water

1. Place the *tofu* in a shallow dish. Mix the oil, ginger, spring onion and
   garlic and pour over the top. Leave to stand until required.

2. Meanwhile make the sauce by melting the creamed coconut in a pan
   over a gentle heat with the soy sauce and lemon juice. Beat in the
   peanut butter and sufficient water to give a thin cream. Heat gently
   until the sauce is of the required thickness, adding more water if
   necessary.

3. Blanch the peppers and fennel by plunging into boiling water for 4-5
   minutes. Drain and thread on to four skewers with the *tofu* and
   prunes. Place under a medium grill and cook for 6-8 minutes, turning
   from time to time.

Vegetarian *Thali*

———◆———

In India a selection of curried vegetable dishes is often served as a vegetarian *thali* or platter. The dishes are served in small stainless steel bowls on a stainless steel tray. Choose from Okra Tamatar (see below), Tarka Dhal (see page 97), Spiced Potatoes or Aloo Gobi (see pages 85 and 101), Vegetable Curry (see page 141) and Aloo Kofta (see below), together with rice and pickles.

Okra Tamatar

4 tablespoons oil
225g (8oz) okra, cut into 2.5cm
  (1in) pieces
2 fresh green chillies, seeded and
  finely sliced

1 can of Rogan Josh curry sauce
salt
2 tomatoes

1. Fry the okra and chillies together in the oil for 5 minutes, turning occasionally. Add the Rogan Josh sauce and salt to taste. Simmer for 3 minutes.

2. Chop the tomatoes and add to the sauce. Mix well and serve.

Aloo Kofta

450g (1lb) potatoes, peeled, boiled
  and mashed
1 tablespoon mild curry paste
salt to taste
50g (2oz) flaked almonds, toasted
  and chopped
1 teaspoon fennel seeds, crushed
2 teaspoons fresh chopped
  coriander
plain flour
oil for deep-frying

Sauce
4 tablespoons oil
1 medium onion, peeled and finely
  chopped
2 tomatoes, finely chopped
$^{1}/_{2}$ teaspoon puréed fresh ginger
$^{1}/_{2}$ teaspoon garlic purée
1 sachet Kashmir mild curry sauce
  mix
150ml ($^{1}/_{4}$ pint) water

1. Add the curry paste, salt, almonds, fennel seeds and coriander to the mashed potato and mix well.

2. Divide the mixture into eight. Flour your hands and work each piece into an oval tube shape.

140

3. Deep fry in moderately hot oil for approximately 5 minutes or until brown.

4. For the sauce, gently fry the onion, tomatoes, ginger, garlic and curry sauce mix for 5 minutes. Add the water and stir until the mixture thickens. Pour over the kofta balls and serve.

Vegetable Curry

Serve this easy-to-make but tasty curry with rice, Raita and Tarka Dhal (see pages 169 and 97), or as part of a Vegetarian Thali (see opposite).

3 tablespoons vegetable oil
1 large onion, peeled and finely
* chopped*
3 garlic cloves, peeled and chopped
700g (1¹/₂lb) mixed vegetables
* (carrots, cauliflower florets,*
* courgettes, aubergines and*
* potatoes)*
2.5cm (1in) piece fresh root ginger,
* peeled and grated*
1 tablespoon ground cumin

1 tablespoon ground coriander
salt and freshly ground black
* pepper*
150ml (¹/₄ pint) water
225g (8oz) peas
3-4 tablespoons freshly chopped
* green coriander*
1 teaspoon garam masala *or curry*
* powder*
juice of ¹/₂ lemon
3 tomatoes, quartered

1. Heat the oil in a pan and fry the onion and garlic until lightly browned. Add the vegetables and stir well. Add the ginger, spices and seasonings and cook until the vegetables are lightly browned all over.

2. Pour on the water and bring to the boil. Simmer for 30 minutes.

3. Add all the remaining ingredients except the tomatoes. Stir and return to the boil.

4. Place the tomato quarters on the top. Cover and simmer for another 10 minutes.

Red Pepper *Gougère*
— ◆ —

The choux pastry for the *gougère* is much easier to make than you might think. The secret lies in beating in the eggs as quickly as possible. Don't worry if the mixture is a little loose.

If you cannot find red peppers, green ones can be used instead. The result will be equally good but not quite so sweet. If you do not want to use cheese just leave it out.

SERVES 4-6

150ml (¹/₄ pint) water
125g (4oz) butter
125g (4oz) plain flour
a pinch of salt
4 eggs
75g (3oz) Gruyère cheese, grated
1 tablespoon grated Parmesan cheese

Filling
1 large onion, peeled and sliced
1 tablespoon cooking oil

a knob of butter
2 large red peppers, seeded and cut into strips
1 tablespoon tomato purée
1 large continental tomato, peeled and chopped
1 tablespoon freshly chopped parsley
freshly chopped rosemary or basil
salt and freshly ground black pepper

1. To prepare the filling, fry the onion in oil and butter until it turns transparent. Add the pepper strips and continue frying gently for a further 3-4 minutes. Add all the remaining filling ingredients and simmer for 20-30 minutes until thick and tender. Remove the lid and boil to reduce any excess liquid. Leave to cool.

2. Preheat the oven to 220°C/425°F/Gas 7.

3. To make the *gougère*, heat the water and butter in a saucepan. When the butter melts bring the mixture to the boil and beat in the flour and salt. Remove from the heat when the mixture starts to come away from the sides of the pan. Beat the eggs in, one at a time, and continue beating until the mixture is satin smooth. Beat in the Gruyère cheese.

4. Use the *gougère* mixture to line the sides of an oval, heatproof entrée dish, leaving the centre base clear. Fill this hollow with the pepper mixture, sprinkle with Parmesan and bake for 1 hour, 10 minutes. Check after 50 minutes, and cover with foil for the last 15 minutes cooking time if browning too quickly.

Avocado Risotto with Mexican Sauce

——◆——

The contrasting colours and flavours of this dish make an unusual main course for a dinner party. Serve a tossed green salad with olive oil and lemon juice on the side.

1 large onion, peeled and finely chopped
1 tablespoon olive oil
350g (12oz) Italian risotto rice
300ml (1/2 pint) white wine
2 avocados, peeled, stoned and chopped
50g (2oz) raisins
1/2 teaspoon mixed herbs
salt and freshly ground black pepper
600ml (1 pint) vegetable stock (see page xii)

Mexican sauce
1 red pepper, seeded and finely chopped
1 green pepper, seeded and finely chopped
1 garlic clove, peeled and crushed
1 tablespoon cooking oil
8 tomatoes, chopped
1 teaspoon ground coriander
2 cloves
1/2 teaspoon chilli powder
300ml (1/2 pint) vegetable stock or water

1. Start by making the sauce. Fry the peppers and garlic in the cooking oil for 5 minutes. Add all the other sauce ingredients plus some salt and pepper, and bring to the boil. Simmer for 20 minutes. Liquidise and correct seasoning if necessary.

2. To make the risotto, fry the onion in the olive oil until transparent. Add the rice and continue frying gently for 3-4 minutes. Add the wine and bring to the boil. Continue cooking until all the wine is absorbed, stirring from time to time.

3. Add avocado, raisins, herbs, seasoning and vegetable stock. Continue cooking until the rice has absorbed all the stock (about 20-30 minutes). Stir from time to time. Add more stock if the rice shows signs of drying out too much.

4. Reheat the sauce and serve with the risotto.

Ratatouille Roulade

—◆—

The 'soufflé'-like mixture bakes to a firm rectangle which is not difficult to roll once the ratatouille filling is in place. It looks wonderful, and is a really effective dish to serve at a dinner party.

Ratatouille filling
225g (8oz) onions, peeled and chopped
225g (8oz) courgettes, trimmed and sliced
225g (8oz) tomatoes, chopped
1 aubergine, diced
1 green pepper, seeded and diced
1 tablespoon cooking oil
2 tablespoons tomato purée
150ml (¹/₄ pint) dry white wine

¹/₂ teaspoon dried oregano
¹/₂ tablespoon flour

Roulade
15g (¹/₂oz) butter
15g (¹/₂oz) flour
150ml (¹/₄ pint) milk
5 eggs, separated
salt and freshly ground black pepper

1. For the filling, gently fry all the vegetables together in the cooking oil. After 3-4 minutes add the tomato purée, wine, herb and some salt and pepper, and bring to the boil. Sprinkle on the flour and stir. Cook for about 30 minutes until all the vegetables are soft and most of the liquid has been taken up.

2. Preheat the oven to 200°C/400°F/Gas 6, and line a 25 × 35cm (10 × 14in) Swiss roll tin with baking paper. Oil the paper well.

3. For the roulade, place the butter, flour and milk in a saucepan and whisk over gentle heat until the mixture thickens. Beat well, and add the egg yolks and seasoning.

4. Next whisk the egg whites until really stiff. Carefully fold into the roulade base and pour into the lined tin. Bake for 15 minutes.

5. Remove from the oven and pour two-thirds of the ratatouille mixture over the roulade. Roll up, removing the greaseproof paper as you go. Serve with remaining ratatouille on either side.

Asparagus Pancake Stack

——◆——

I find that this is a good dinner party dish because I can make both the pancakes and the fillings well in advance. They are then reheated in the oven or microwave and very quickly put together before serving. The dish also looks very impressive!

125g (4oz) plain flour
salt
2 eggs, separated
300ml (¹/₂ pint) milk
cooking oil
freshly chopped parsley

Fillings
40g (1¹/₂oz) plain flour
40g (1¹/₂oz) butter

1 × 350g (12oz) can of asparagus, drained and chopped (keep the liquid)
milk
150ml (¹/₄ pint) dry white wine
freshly ground black pepper
225g (8oz) mushrooms, finely chopped
2 tablespoons cooking oil

1. Start by making the pancakes. In a bowl, mix the flour, salt, egg yolks and milk. Whisk the egg whites until really stiff and fold into the flour mixture. Grease a 20cm (8in) frying pan with oil and heat. Spoon a quarter of the batter into the hot pan to make a thick pancake. Cook until golden then turn over and cook the other side. Repeat to make three more pancakes. Keep warm while you make the fillings.

2. For the fillings, place the flour and butter in a pan. Measure the liquid from the can of asparagus and make up to about 600ml (1 pint) with milk. Add to the flour and butter and whisk over a medium heat until thickened. Add the wine and season to taste with salt and pepper. The sauce should be fairly thick.

3. Divide the sauce in two and add the chopped asparagus to one-half. Fry the mushrooms in the cooking oil and add to the other half of the sauce.

4. To make the stack, lay one pancake on a serving dish and cover with half the mushroom sauce. Add another pancake and cover with half the asparagus sauce. Continue with alternate layers ending with asparagus. Decorate with parsley and serve at once. Cut like a cake.

BUFFET FOOD

———◆———

Choose two or three of the pastry-based dishes in this section, and team them up with a selection of salads for a really impressive buffet. Ideas include Watercress Flan and Savoury Pumpkin Plait with Rice Cake, Carrot and Fennel Coleslaw and Sala Beetroot Salad; Pâtes de Béziers and Onion and Black Olive Tart with Cauliflower and Grilled Red Pepper Salad and Mixed Leaf and Pistachio Nut Salad; or St Christopher Savoury Roll and Celeriac and Carrot Flan with Rainbow Pasta Salad, Cauliflower Salad and Wholemeal Rolls.

A good winter buffet includes Hot Cauliflower Terrine, Smoked *Tofu* Kedgeree and Mexican Baked Spinach; or Indian Chickpeas, Singapore Rice and Roman-Style Spinach.

All the pasta and stir-fry dishes in earlier chapters can be increased in volume and served as buffet food. Finish off with a large bowl of fruits in season.

Cheese Log

———◆———

My mother used to make this with our local Lancashire cheese which in those days had a good tang to it. Today it is mostly very mild indeed, and this dish is best made with Leicestershire cheese for its colour, or any well-flavoured, firm, mature cheese.

SERVES 16

700g (1¹/₂lb) cheese, grated (see above)
350g (12oz) carrots or celeriac, peeled and grated
6 tablespoons freshly chopped spring onion
4 tablespoons freshly chopped parsley

6 tablespoons mayonnaise
salt and freshly ground black pepper
sprigs of fresh herbs and cherry tomatoes to decorate

1. Mix the cheese with the carrot or celeriac, the spring onion, parsley, mayonnaise and seasoning.

2. Spoon the mixture down the centre of a large rectangle of baking paper and roll up into a log shape. Place in the fridge to cool for an hour.

3. Carefully remove the paper and serve on a long serving dish, decorated with sprigs of fresh herbs and cherry tomatoes. Cut into slices to serve.

Watercress Flan

——◆——

Cook the flan base in advance, and fill just before serving. Cottage cheese or grated Cheddar can also be used in place of *tofu*.

SERVES 12

350g (12oz) shortcrust pastry
2 bunches of watercress
8 celery sticks trimmed and
  chopped
a bunch of spring onions, finely
  chopped

450g (1lb) tofu, mashed
3-4 tablespoons mayonnaise
salt and freshly ground black
  pepper
125g (4oz) shelled walnuts, halved

1. Preheat the oven to 200°C/400°F/Gas 6.

2. Roll out the pastry and use to line two 20cm (8in) flan tins. Prick the bases all over with a fork and line with foil and dried beans. Bake blind for about 15 minutes then remove the foil and beans. Cook for a further 15 minutes until cooked. Remove from the oven and leave to cool.

3. Pick out about a dozen sprigs of watercress from the bunches and reserve for garnish. Coarsely chop the rest, and use to line the cold pastry cases.

4. Mix the celery with the spring onion, *tofu*, mayonnaise and seasoning. Spoon into the centre of the flans leaving a little of the watercress showing round the edges.

5. Place the walnuts round the edges on top of the watercress, and decorate the centre with the reserved sprigs of watercress. Serve at once.

147

Pâtes de Béziers

———◆———

These attractive little tartlets from the Languedoc can be made with almost any kind of dough. In France they are usually covered with pastry lids, but these open versions look more attractive on the buffet table. They can be served hot or cold.

MAKES 16

Pastry
175g (6oz) butter or firm
   margarine
300g (10oz) plain white flour
$^1/_2$ teaspoon salt
1 egg (size 1), beaten
2 tablespoons water

Chèvre tomato filling
225g (8oz) chèvre roulade
4 tablespoons goat's milk yoghurt
1 egg
leaves from 2-3 sprigs of fresh
   thyme

salt and freshly ground black
   pepper
3 tomatoes, sliced

Onion filling
450g (1lb) onions, peeled and
   sliced
2 tablespoons olive oil
1 egg (size 1), beaten
175g (6oz) low-fat fromage frais or
   quark
$^1/_2$ teaspoon dried sage

1. To make the pastry, rub the fat into the flour and salt until the mixture resembles rough breadcrumbs. Bind with the beaten egg and water. Leave to rest in the fridge for 2 hours.

2. Roll out and use to line sixteen 10cm (4in) tartlet tins.

3. Preheat the oven to 190°C/375°F/Gas 5.

4. To make the *chèvre* filling, cut the rind off the cheese and beat with the yoghurt to make a smooth cream. Then beat in the egg, thyme and seasoning.

5. Place slices of tomato in the base of eight of the prepared flan tins, and spoon the cheese mixture over the top. Bake for 35 minutes.

6. To make the onion filling, fry the onions in the oil until they soften. Beat the egg and *fromage frais* together and stir in the onion, sage and some salt and pepper. Spoon into the remaining eight prepared pastry cases and bake for 35 minutes.

Celeriac and Carrot Flan

—◆—

This potato pastry can be used for any kind of quiche or savoury tart. For the best results chill the pastry for half an hour before cooking.

SERVES 6-8

Potato pastry
50g (2oz) firm margarine
75g (3oz) cold mashed potato
100g (3¹/₂oz) wholemeal flour
1 teaspoon baking powder
a pinch of salt

Filling
200g (7oz) celeriac, peeled and
   sliced

1 large carrot, peeled and grated
3 eggs
150g (5oz) Greek yoghurt
50ml (2fl oz) skimmed milk
50g (2oz) Cheddar cheese, grated
salt and freshly ground black
   pepper

1. Preheat the oven to 190°C/375°F/Gas 5.

2. To make the pastry, cream the margarine with the back of a spoon to soften it. Then use a fork to work in the cold potato, flour, baking powder and salt. Blend well together and turn on to a floured board. Knead slightly and roll out to fill the base of a 20cm (8in) loose-based flan tin. Work the pastry up the sides of the flan with your fingers and, if time allows, place in the fridge for half an hour.

2. For the filling, cook the celeriac in boiling water for 10 minutes. Drain and grate. Mix with the grated carrot. Beat the eggs, yoghurt and milk together and stir in the cheese, vegetables and seasoning.

3. Spoon into the flan base, spread evenly and bake for about 45 minutes until set in the centre and golden brown.

Onion and Black Olive Tart

—◆—

This well-flavoured tart from Provence makes a good buffet dish. It is traditionally made with a yeast dough. However, if you are in a hurry the pastry is quicker to make. I give recipes for both below.

SERVES 6-8

Yeast dough base
300g (10oz) plain flour
1/2 teaspoon salt
1 1/2 teaspoons activated dried yeast
2 1/2 tablespoons olive oil
150-165ml (5-5 1/2fl oz) lukewarm
    water

Alternative pastry dough base
75g (3oz) butter
200g (7oz) plain flour

1/4 teaspoon salt
50-75ml (2-3fl oz) water

Topping
3 tablespoons olive oil
1.5kg (3lb) onions, peeled and
    sliced
salt and freshly ground black
    pepper
24 black olives

1. If you are making the yeast dough base, mix the flour with the salt and yeast. Add the oil and sufficient water to make a fairly stiff dough. Knead on a floured surface for 10 minutes then leave to rise in a warm place in a greased mixing bowl covered with clingfilm.

2. If you are making the pastry dough base, rub the butter into the flour and salt until the mixture resembles breadcrumbs. Bind with the water and knead lightly to form a dough.

3. To make the topping, heat the oil in a pan and add the onions. Stir until the onions soften, then leave to cook over a low heat. The onions should not brown, but in about 40 minutes will slowly melt to a golden purée. Season to taste.

4. Preheat the oven to 220°C/425°F/Gas 7.

5. Roll out your chosen dough and use to line a 25cm (10in) flan dish or tin. Spoon the onion mixture into the flan, dot with olives and bake in the preheated oven for 30-35 minutes, until the base is cooked through.

Savoury Pumpkin Plait

——◆——

The smoked *tofu* gives a very distinctive flavour to this attractive puff pastry buffet dish. If you cannot find any pumpkins, use a mixture of swede, to give the same colour, and marrow to give a similar taste.

SERVES 8-10

175g (6oz) smoked tofu, diced
175g (6oz) pumpkin flesh or
marrow and swede flesh, diced
1 small onion, peeled and chopped
175g (6oz) potatoes, peeled and
diced
1 small carrot, peeled and diced
3 tablespoons frozen peas
1 teaspoon dried mixed herbs

1 tablespoon freshly chopped
parsley
salt and freshly ground black
pepper
2 tablespoons cooking oil
1 × 375g (13oz) packet of frozen
puff pastry, thawed
beaten egg to glaze the pastry

1. Preheat the oven to 220°C/425°F/Gas 7.

2. Mix the *tofu* with the diced and chopped vegetables, peas, herbs and seasoning. Heat the oil in a pan and gently fry the vegetable mixture for 8 minutes.

3. Roll out the pastry to approximately 33 × 28cm (13 × 11in) and trim to a neat oblong. Arrange the cooked vegetables down the centre leaving 10cm (4in) of pastry clear at each side. Make slanting cuts into the base pastry on each side, about 2.5cm (1in) apart. Criss-cross these pieces alternately to enclose the filling. Neaten the ends and place on a baking sheet.

4. Brush with beaten egg and bake for a further 20 minutes. Reduce the heat to 180°C/350°F/Gas 4 and cook for a further 15 minutes.

St Christopher Savoury Roll

—◆—

This was one of the first dishes I ever learned to cook at school, and I am still using it as a centrepiece for a hot buffet. Two of these rolls will serve ten to twelve people with other dishes.

Filling
200g (7oz) mature Cheddar cheese, grated
2 onions, peeled and finely chopped
2 tablespoons tomato purée
freshly ground black pepper

Pastry
75g (3oz) butter
200g (7oz) plain flour
a pinch of salt
water

1. Preheat the oven to 200°C/400°F/Gas 6.

2. Mix all the filling ingredients together, with a little salt, and keep on one side.

3. For the pastry, rub the fat into the flour and salt to make a breadcrumb texture. Bind with a little water. Roll out to a 25 × 30cm (10 × 12in) rectangle.

4. Spread the cheese mixture all over the pastry, leaving a small margin clear round the edges. Roll up the pastry and filling from a longer side, to give a flattish Swiss roll. Place on an oiled baking tray in a crescent shape.

5. Cut across the roll, leaving the pastry uncut at one side, to make about 12 sections. Starting from one end, partially twist each of the twelve sections to expose the spiral filling. Bake for about 25-30 minutes. Serve hot or cold.

Cardamom Cheese Pie

—◆—

The filling for this dish was inspired by very typical Chilean flavours – the raisins, sugar and eggs – and they work very well indeed in this party pie.

SERVES 8-10

Filling
8 hard-boiled eggs, shelled
350g (12oz) Cheddar cheese,
    grated
225g (8oz) raisins
2 tablespoons sugar
crushed seeds from 2 cardamom
    pods

Pastry
125g (4oz) butter
225g (8oz) plain flour
a pinch of salt
water

1. Preheat the oven to 200°C/400°F/Gas 6.

2. For the pastry, rub the fat into the flour and salt, and bind with a little water. Roll out and use three-quarters to line two 20cm (8in) flan tins.

3. Chop the hard-boiled eggs and mix with the remaining filling ingredients. Spoon into the pastry bases.

4. Roll out the remaining pastry to make lids. Put these on, fork the edges and prick the centre. Bake for 45 minutes or until the pastry is cooked.

Rice Cake

—◆—

This colourful rice salad looks very good turned out on to a serving dish surrounded with watercress.

SERVES 12

450g (1lb) long-grain rice
300ml (1/2 pint) soured cream
225g (8oz) cooked beetroot,
    skinned
4 hard-boiled eggs, shelled and
    chopped

75g (3oz) roasted peanuts, chopped
salt and freshly ground black
    pepper
1/2 bunch watercress

1. Cook the rice in double its volume of boiling salted water. Drain well and fluff up with a fork. Stir in the soured cream and leave to cool.

2. Grate the beetroot and mix with chopped hard-boiled eggs and peanuts. Mix with the cooled rice.

3. Pack into a loaf tin and weight the top. Chill well, unmould, and serve garnished with watercress.

Vegetable Terrine

—◆—

This terrine is as colourful as it is delicious. It looks great on a buffet, or it can be served as the first course at a special dinner.

SERVES 8

450g (1lb) carrots, peeled and
    chopped
450g (1lb) parsnips, peeled and
    chopped
25g (1oz) butter
1 medium onion, peeled and
    chopped
6 eggs
4 tablespoons Greek strained
    yoghurt

salt and freshly ground white
    pepper
1kg (2lb) fresh spinach, tough
    stalks removed or 450g (1lb)
    frozen chopped spinach
$1/2$ teaspoon freshly grated nutmeg
2 tablespoons freshly chopped
    chives

1. Put the carrots and parsnips into separate saucepans, with enough boiling water to half cover the vegetables. Cook until *al dente*. Drain both well.

2. In a small pan melt the butter, add the onion, and cook until soft.

3. In a bowl beat 2 eggs with 2 tablespoons of yoghurt, season with salt and pepper and whisk together until smooth.

4. Drain the carrots, put into a food processor or blender with half of the cooked onions, and purée to the stage where the mixture is still fairly coarse. Turn into a bowl and stir into the egg and yoghurt. Spoon this carrot mixture into the base of a well greased 1.5 litre ($2^1/2$ pint) loaf tin.

5. Repeat the same procedure with the parsnips, using the rest of the onion, 2 eggs and the remaining yoghurt, then carefully spoon over the carrot layer.

6. Preheat the oven to 180°C/350°F/Gas 4.

7. Put the fresh spinach into a large saucepan of water, place over a medium high heat and cook for a few minutes until wilted. Turn into a colander and squeeze out as much water as possible. Either finely chop on a board or in a food processor.

8. Add the remaining beaten eggs, the nutmeg and chives to the chopped spinach and season well with salt and pepper. Spoon this mixture over the parsnip layer then cover with a piece of well buttered greaseproof paper.

9. Place the loaf tin in an ovenproof dish and pour in enough water to three-quarters fill the dish. Cook in the oven for 1¼ hours. Allow to cool for 10 minutes before turning out. Slice carefully to serve.

Hot Cauliflower Terrine
——◆——

This was one of the first vegetarian dishes I ever tried out on my meat-eating friends, and they could not believe that vegetarian food could be so good!

SERVES 8-10

2 cauliflowers
2 onions, peeled and chopped
25g (1oz) butter or firm margarine
175g (6oz) fresh breadcrumbs
300ml (½ pint) soured cream

4 eggs, beaten
grated nutmeg
salt and freshly ground black
  pepper
fresh chopped parsley

1. Preheat the oven to 190°C/375°F/Gas 5, and grease a large casserole or soufflé dish.

2. Remove the outer leaves and excess stalks from the cauliflowers and steam until tender. Drain well and mash to a purée.

3. Fry the onion in butter until soft. Mix into the mashed cauliflower, breadcrumbs, soured cream, eggs, nutmeg and seasoning.

4. Spoon the mixture into the prepared casserole or soufflé dish and bake for 1 hour. Sprinkle the top with freshly chopped parsley and serve at once.

155

Smoked *Tofu* Kedgeree

——◆——

If you do not want to include eggs, substitute 450g (1lb) of cooked vegetables such as cubed celeriac or chopped artichoke hearts, with some diced carrots or sweetcorn for colour.

SERVES 8 or more, with other dishes

125g (4oz) butter or firm
  margarine
700g (1¹/₂lb) cooked long-grain
  brown rice
700g (1¹/₂ lb) smoked tofu, cubed
6 hard-boiled eggs, shelled and
  chopped

a pinch of curry powder
salt and freshly ground black
  pepper
250ml (8fl oz) soured cream or
  puréed silken tofu
8 tablespoons freshly chopped
  parsley

1. Heat the butter in a deep saucepan and toss the rice in this until thoroughly coated. Add the *tofu* and eggs (or vegetables), and fold carefully into the rice.

2. Mix the remaining ingredients in a cup and pour over the kedgeree. Carefully toss over the heat to warm through and serve at once.

Mexican Baked Spinach

——◆——

This is a favourite of mine for buffet parties. Serve with Texan Rice (see page 63), Stewed beetroot with Onions (see page 90) and another vegetable dish of your choice.

SERVES 12

1.25kg (2³/₄lb) spinach, tough
  stalks removed
4 green peppers, seeded and sliced
2 large onions, peeled and finely
  chopped
¹/₂ head celery, trimmed and finely
  chopped
2 tablespoons cooking oil

125g (4oz) raisins
1 teaspoon ground cinnamon
¹/₂ teaspoon cayenne pepper
¹/₂ teaspoon dill seeds
150ml (¹/₄ pint) tomato juice
225g (8oz) cheese, grated
salt and freshly ground black
  pepper

1. Preheat the oven to 190°C/375°F/Gas 5.

2. Wash and drain the spinach and steam in a large pan with no added water for 5 minutes until soft. Blanch the green peppers for 5 minutes in boiling water.

3. Fry the onions and celery in cooking oil with the raisins, cinnamon, cayenne and dill seed for 5 minutes.

4. Place half the spinach in the base of a large oval earthenware dish. Season and sprinkle with a little tomato juice. Add a layer of peppers and then all the onion and celery mixture. Season and sprinkle with more tomato juice and half the cheese. Cover with the remaining peppers. Next add the remaining spinach and season and sprinkle with the remaining tomato juice. Top with grated cheese.

5. Bake for 45 minutes.

Indian Chickpeas
—◆—

This dish is based on an old recipe from Delhi. It can be made hotter by the addition of fresh green chilli.

SERVES 8-10

3 tablespoons vegetable oil
2 teaspoons whole coriander seeds
1 teaspoon whole cumin seeds
1 onion, peeled and sliced
2 garlic cloves, peeled and chopped
2 teaspoons ground coriander
1 teaspoon each of ground cumin
  and turmeric

1 × 400g (14oz) can of tomatoes
2 teaspoons paprika
1 teaspoon salt
2 × 400g (14oz) cans of chickpeas,
  drained
1 teaspoon freshly grated root
  ginger

1. Heat the oil in a heavy-based saucepan and fry the whole spices for 1 minute. Add the onion and garlic and continue frying for 2-3 minutes.

2. Next add the ground spices. Stir and add all the remaining ingredients except the ginger. Bring the mixture to the boil, cover and simmer for 20 minutes.

3. Add the ginger and cook for a further 5 minutes until fairly thick.

Rainbow Pasta Salad

—◆—

Use a packet of three-coloured and flavoured pasta spirals for the best effect.

SERVES 10

225g (8oz) mixed plain, tomato
    and spinach pasta spirals
salt
4¹/₂ tablespoons olive oil
1 tablespoon cider or white wine
    vinegar
1 bunch of spring onions, finely
    chopped

1 green pepper, seeded and diced
1 red pepper, seeded and diced
3 tablespoons cooked sweetcorn
a pinch of mixed dried herbs
freshly ground black pepper
8 black olives, stoned and halved

1. Cook the pasta spirals as directed on the pack in plenty of boiling salted water with 1 teaspoon of the oil. When they are just tender to the bite, drain very well.

2. Toss in the rest of the oil and the vinegar and leave to cool.

3. Add all the remaining ingredients. Toss well and serve.

FINGER FOOD

◆

This section includes the recipes for some of my favourite finger food. Indeed I like some of the recipes so much I make them for everything from dinner party appetisers to everyday snacks! The pâtés and spreads also make good sandwich fillings or toppings for toasted bread.

A good selection of canapés for a two-hour drinks party includes Green Goddess Dip with Celery, Peanut and Garlic Pâté Canapés, Chopped Egg and Onion on Rye, Cheese Dreams, Aïoli in Mushroom Caps and Sesame Balls. A more substantial finger-food menu for an evening party includes Guacamole with Potato Skins, Mali Canapés, Stuffed Eggs, Chinese Money Bags, *Tofu* Cakes with Sweet-Sour Sauce and Spiced Lentil Tartlets.

Peanut and Garlic Pâté

— ◆ —

This makes a good spread for fried bread canapés. Top some with capers and others with diced tomato or sliced stuffed olives.

MAKES 24-30 canapés

3 tablespoons peanut butter
125g (4oz) soft cheese
2-3 garlic cloves, peeled and finely
   chopped

2 tablespoons plain yoghurt
a few drops of Tabasco sauce
salt and freshly ground black
   pepper

1. Place all the ingredients in a bowl and mix together with a fork until well blended.

2. Store in the fridge until required.

Green Goddess Dip with Celery

—◆—

The Americans are very keen on dips and this recipe came from a friend in Washington. If you use a little less mayonnaise you can spread the mixture directly on to the sticks of celery instead of serving as a dip.

SERVES 20

6-8 young spinach leaves
225g (8oz) low-fat soft cheese
2½ tablespoons mayonnaise
1 garlic clove, peeled and crushed
chopped green tips from a bunch of
    spring onions

freshly chopped parsley
salt and freshly ground black
    pepper
2 heads of celery, washed and
    trimmed

1. Very finely shred the spinach and then chop it.

2. Mix with the cheese and mayonnaise. Stir in the garlic, spring onion and parsley, and season to taste.

3. Spoon into a bowl and serve with trimmed lengths of celery.

Mali Canapés

—◆—

Plain or smoked *tofu* can be used very successfully in place of cheese in this African-inspired recipe.

MAKES 40

125g (4oz) Cheddar cheese, grated
50g (2oz) roasted peanuts, chopped
25g (1oz) raisins, chopped
2 tablespoons mayonnaise

salt and freshly ground black
    pepper
8 rounds of toast
chopped parsley

1. Mix together all the ingredients except the toast and parsley. Chill for an hour.

2. Spread on to rounds of toast. Cut each piece into six squares and serve sprinkled with chopped parsley.

Guacamole with Potato Skins

—◆—

Make plenty of this, as it is extremely popular! Stop the top of the Guacamole from discolouring by not stinting on the lemon juice and keeping well covered with clingfilm until the very last minute. It is the exposure to air that turns the avocado flesh black. Incidentally, the idea that leaving the avocado stone in the purée will somehow help to stop the change in colour is just not true, so throw the stones away.

SERVES 20

8 large potatoes, baked in the oven
melted butter or cooking oil

Guacamole
juice of 2 lemons
3 ripe tomatoes, finely chopped
1 small onion, peeled and finely
* chopped*

a small bunch of fresh coriander,
* finely chopped*
salt and freshly ground black
* pepper*
Tabasco sauce to taste
3 large ripe avocados

1. Prehead the oven to 200°C/400°F/Gas 6.

2. Cut each of the potatoes into six wedges and remove most of the flesh (reserve for use in Cheese Nut Patties, see page 106). Brush the potato skins with butter or oil and place on a baking sheet. Cook in the oven for about 10 minutes until they are crisp. Turn regularly.

3. To make the Guacamole, mix half the lemon juice in a bowl with all the ingredients except the avocados and chill until required.

4. At the last moment, peel and stone the avocados. Mash the flesh and remaining lemon juice with a fork or purée in a blender or food processor and stir into the tomato and onion mixture. Serve immediately with the hot potato skins.

Sesame Balls

—◆—

These highly nutritious cocktail bites, whose base is Feta cheese and a variety of ground seeds, can be made in advance and stored in the fridge. However, it is not a good idea to leave them overnight as they tend to dry out.

MAKES 40

125g (4oz) sesame seeds
125g (4oz) sunflower seeds
125g (4oz) pumpkin seeds
125g (4oz) Feta cheese

4 teaspoons soy sauce
4 teaspoons sesame oil
2 egg whites, beaten
alfalfa or cress

1. Preheat the oven to 200°C/400°F/Gas 6.

2. Spread the sesame seeds on a baking tray and toast in the oven for 5-6 minutes, turning once or twice with a wooden spoon.

3. Place the sunflower and pumpkin seeds in a food processor and blend until they are smooth and almost creamy. Turn out into a bowl.

4. Add the Feta cheese, soy sauce and sesame oil to the bowl and mix.

5. Shape into 40 small balls. Dip each ball in egg white and then in sesame seeds. Serve on a bed of alfalfa or cress.

Chinese Money Bags

—◆—

Serve these crunchy wontons with their mouth-watering filling as canapés, or as part of a finger buffet. Three or four can also be served as an unusual dinner-party starter with home-made chutney. Vegans might use smoked *tofu* instead of blue cheese.

MAKES 24

4 sheets filo pastry
cooking oil for deep-frying

Filling
150g (5oz) blue Brie, rind removed

50g (2oz) walnut halves, chopped
6 spring onions, chopped
finely grated rind of 1 orange

1. Cut each sheet of filo pastry into twelve 10cm (4in) squares and brush very lightly with water. Arrange in pairs so you have 24 doubled wrappers.

2. To make the filling, mix all the ingredients in a bowl.

3. Place a teaspoon of the filling on each double filo pastry square. Damp the edges again, if necessary, and pinch together into money bag shapes.

4. Heat the oil in a deep fat-fryer, and check the temperature by dropping a 2.5cm (1in) cube of stale bread into the oil – it should brown in 1 minute. Drop the money bags into the hot oil in batches of five or six and cook for 2-3 minutes until crisp and golden. Drain on kitchen paper and serve as quickly as possible.

163

Chopped Egg and Onion on Rye

—◆—

Use this Jewish favourite to make canapés on squares of rye bread or pumpernickel.

SERVES 24

6 hard-boiled eggs, shelled and
  finely chopped
1 bunch of spring onions, finely
  chopped
2-3 tablespoons soft cheese or
  mayonnaise

a dash of wine vinegar
salt and freshly ground black
  pepper
6 slices of rye or black bread

1. Mix all the ingredients, except the bread, in a bowl and chill until required.

2. Spread on to the pieces of bread and cut into squares.

Curried Bean and Onion Squares

—◆—

Any canned beans can be used for this spicy canapé spread, but soya beans make a particularly firm spread.

MAKES 30

4 small onions, peeled and chopped
3 tablespoons cooking oil
1½ teaspoons curry powder
2 teaspoons ground cumin
2 garlic cloves, peeled and crushed
4 tablespoons water

225g (8oz) cooked soya beans, or
  drained canned haricot beans,
  puréed
7-8 large slices of fried bread
freshly chopped parsley

1. Fry the onions in cooking oil with curry powder, cumin and garlic until transparent. Add water and continue to simmer for 5-8 minutes. Add the puréed beans and mix well. Allow to cool.

2. Spread on fried bread. Cut into squares and serve sprinkled with freshly chopped parsley.

Aïoli in Mushroom Caps
—◆—

This garlic mayonnaise can also be used to stuff cherry tomatoes or celery sticks.

MAKES 25-30

4-6 garlic cloves, peeled and
  crushed
1 egg yolk
600ml (1 pint) olive oil
salt and freshly ground black
  pepper

1 tablespoon lemon juice
1kg (2lb) small cup mushrooms,
  stalks removed
sprigs of fresh parsley

1. Beat the garlic and egg yolk together and very gradually whisk in the oil to make a thick mayonnaise. Stir in the seasoning and lemon juice.

2. Fill the mushrooms with the Aïoli. Decorate with parsley sprigs.

Tortilla Squares
—◆—

This Spanish omelette is packed with vegetables which can make it a bit difficult to eat with the fingers. If you are worried about your carpet add another egg to the mixture to help bind things together.

3 potatoes, peeled
1 onion, peeled
1 tomato
1/2 green pepper, seeded
2 courgettes, trimmed

2 tablespoons cooking oil
6 eggs
salt and freshly ground black
  pepper

1. Dice all the vegetables very finely and fry gently in cooking oil in a 23cm (9in) frying pan for about 5 minutes.

2. Beat the eggs, season and pour over the vegetables. Stir well. Turn the heat down low and leave to set for about 30 minutes.

3. Finish off by browning under the grill for 10-15 minutes. Leave to cool and cut into squares. Serve warm or cold.

Tofu Cakes with Sweet-Sour Sauce

—◆—

Cook these tasty little bites in batches and serve as soon as they are made. Larger cakes can be shallow-fried and served as part of a buffet.

MAKES 24

450g (1lb) plain tofu
a bunch of spring onions, very
    finely chopped
2 tablespoons freshly grated root
    ginger
1 teaspoon grated orange rind
125g (4oz) fresh breadcrumbs
2 tablespoons soy sauce
freshly ground black pepper
4 tablespoons rice, potato or corn
    flour

cooking oil for deep-frying

Sweet-sour sauce
450ml (³/₄ pint) pineapple juice
6 tablespoons cider vinegar
6 tablespoons sherry
3 tablespoons soy sauce
6 tablespoons sugar

1. First make the sauce. Mix all the sauce ingredients together in a pan and bring to the boil. Cook for 6-8 minutes until it begins to thicken a little.

2. Meanwhile mash the *tofu* with a fork and mix in all the remaining ingredients except the flour and oil. Shape into small flat balls or cakes and dust with the flour.

3. Deep-fry in batches in hot oil for 4 minutes. Serve hot with the sweet-sour sauce.

Spiced Lentil Tartlets

—◆—

If you do not want to be bothered with making pastry cases, this spicy filling can be piled on to squares of rye bread or small oat biscuits.

MAKES 24

Pastry
125g (4oz) butter or firm
   margarine
225g (8oz) plain flour
a pinch of salt
water

Filling
1 tablespoon cooking oil
1 large onion, peeled and finely
   chopped
1 garlic clove, peeled and finely
   chopped

1 tablespoon tomato purée
1/2 teaspoon chilli powder
1/4 teaspoon ground cumin
1/2 teaspoon dried thyme
1/4 teaspoon allspice
salt and freshly ground black
   pepper
125g (4oz) dried split lentils
600ml (1 pint) water
1 teaspoon yeast extract

1. For the filling, heat the oil in a pan and fry the onion, garlic, tomato purée, spices and seasoning for 5 minutes. Add the lentils and cover with the water and yeast extract. Bring to the boil and simmer for about 1-1½ hours until the lentils are cooked and the mixture is fairly thick.

2. Preheat the oven to 200°C/400°F/Gas 6.

3. Meanwhile make the pastry by rubbing the fat into the flour and salt until the mixture resembles fine breadcrumbs. Bind with water. Roll out three-quarters of the pastry and use to line 24 small tartlet tins. Roll out the remaining pastry to make lids.

4. Place a spoonful of the filling in each tartlet and cover with a pastry lid. Pinch closed. Bake for about 35-40 minutes until lightly browned. Serve hot.

Stuffed Eggs
—◆—

Stuffed eggs are always popular finger food. I like to make two or three different stuffings and mix them on a platter. Quantities of each filling are for six hard-boiled eggs.

1. Watercress

a bunch of watercress, well picked over
125ml (4fl oz) mayonnaise

salt and freshly ground black pepper

1. Remove the egg yolks and rub through a sieve. Finely chop the watercress, retaining a few sprigs for decoration. Add the chopped watercress to the egg yolks with the mayonnaise and seasoning and mix well together.

2. Spoon back into the whites and garnish with a few sprigs of watercress.

2. Curried Onion

2 tablespoons cooking oil
1 small onion, peeled and finely chopped
1 tablespoon curry powder

2 tablespoons mango chutney, chopped if necessary
mayonnaise
sprigs of parsley

1. Heat the oil in a pan and fry the onion for 4-5 minutes until well browned. Stir in the curry powder and cook for another 2 minutes. Leave to cool.

2. Mix with the sieved egg yolks, chutney and a little mayonnaise to bind.

3. Spoon back into the whites and garnish with a few sprigs of parsley.

3. Provençale

$^1/_2$ × 50g (2oz) jar of black olive
  paste
1 tablespoon capers, drained and
  chopped

a few whole capers, drained

1. Rub the egg yolks through a sieve and mix with the olive paste and chopped capers.
2. Pile back into the egg whites and decorate with a few whole capers.

4. Coriander and *Tahina*

2 tablespoons mayonnaise
1 tablespoon tahina
3 tablespoons freshly chopped
  coriander

salt and freshly ground black
  pepper

1. Mix the mayonnaise with the *tahina* to make a smooth soft paste. Stir in the sieved egg yolks, coriander and seasonings, mixing well.
2. Pile back into the egg whites.

Raita
——◆——

This cooling yogurt dish goes well with both Indian and Middle Eastern dishes. In the latter area garlic is added instead of cumin seeds, and the dish is served as an appetiser with hot pitta bread.

225g (8oz) plain yoghurt
10cm (4 in) piece cucumber, diced
  or coarsely grated
2 tablespoons freshly chopped mint

$^1/_2$ teaspoon ground cumin
$^1/_4$ teaspoon cayenne pepper
salt

1. Whisk the yoghurt to make it really smooth and stir in all the other ingredients. Chill before serving.

Tapenade

—◆—

Though you can buy this olive paste ready made in jars, it is fun to make at home. Serve as a starter or snack with toasted crusty bread.

SERVES 12

350g (12oz) pitted black olives
2 tablespoons capers, drained
2 garlic cloves, peeled and crushed
1 tablespoon Dijon mustard
1 tablespoon lemon juice

200ml (8fl oz) Extra Virgin olive
    oil
freshly ground black pepper
toasted crusty bread, to serve

1. Put all the ingredients except the oil, pepper and bread in a food processor or blender and roughly chop.

2. With the machine still running, gradually add the olive oil. Season to taste with pepper.

3. Spoon into a serving dish and chill well for 1-2 hours. Serve with toasted bread.

Cheese Dreams

—◆—

These simple fried sandwiches are the most popular finger food I have every served. They disappear just as fast as you can make them.

MAKES 40

12 slices of bread
soft butter
450g (1lb) Cheddar cheese, grated

4 tablespoons chutney
salt and freshly ground black
    pepper
butter for frying

1. Butter the bread thinly and mix the cheese and chutney together. Season.

2. Make up six sandwiches with the bread and the cheese mixture. Cut each sandwich into quarters and each quarter into two triangles.

3. Fry each triangle on both sides in hot butter and serve at once.

Orange Cheese Truffles

This combination of dried fruit, orange juice and soft cheese provides something for guests with a sweet tooth.

MAKES 60

225g (8oz) dates
225g (8oz) raisins
150g (6oz) flaked almonds
450g (1lb) soft cream cheese
rind and juice of 1 orange

1 teaspoon mixed spice
3-4 tablespoons toasted ground
  sesame seeds
7 oranges

1. Finely chop the dates, raisins and almonds and mix with the cream cheese. Add mixed spice and the finely grated rind of one orange, together with enough juice from the same orange to make a stiff paste. Mix well and chill for 4-6 hours.

2. Remove from the fridge and shape into about 60 small balls. Roll in toasted ground sesame seeds.

3. To serve, slice remaining oranges into slim wedges and arrange on a large plate with the cheese truffles.

Garlic Sauce with Vegetables

—◆—

This rather unusual Garlic Sauce uses a combination of bread and ground almonds as thickening agents. Serve as a dip as part of a buffet or for a pre-dinner nibble.

SERVES 12

6 slices day-old bread, crusts
  removed
4-6 garlic cloves, peeled and
  crushed
2 tablespoons white wine vinegar
300ml (½ pint) Extra Virgin olive
  oil

50g (2oz) ground almonds
pinch of salt
selection of lightly cooked
  vegetables such as mangetout,
  baby courgettes, spring onions,
  asparagus, cauliflower florets

1. Soak the bread in water for 5 minutes. Squeeze out all the moisture and blend with the garlic and vinegar in a food processor or blender until smooth.

2. Add the olive oil, a few drops at a time. When the mixture starts to thicken, begin to add the olive oil in a thin continuous stream and continue until all the oil has been used. Stir in the ground almonds and season to taste.

3. Spoon into a serving dish and serve with the lightly cooked vegetables.

INDEX

───◆───